Montana....

As I Remember It

Ronald Ivan Johnstad

First Printing...1996
Second Printing..2000

For information, address the Rev. Dr. Ron Johnstad, P.O. Box 981, Emigrant, Montana, 59027.

Tel./FAX - 1-406-333-9003

ISBN No: 0-9670130-1-1

Printed in the U.S.A. by:
HEINS PUBLICATIONS
Rev. William A. Heins
P.O. Box 998
Eau Claire WI 54702-0998
Tel. #'s: 715.874.6677; 800.554.3467

Acknowledgments

A special thanks to Jerry Arthun, a long-time friend of the family, from Clyde Park, Montana, for her work of editing this book, and to Len, her husband, for listening while she read it. Also, a special thanks given to everyone mentioned in the book. To the Montanans who lived the stories...for your character, uniqueness, and your special friendship. Finally, the author thanks his wife, Mary Ellen, for her patience and endurance while all was being written.

Table of Contents

Wilsall and White Sulphur Springs

Livingston

Billings

INTRODUCTION

The 1970s and 1980s were a time of great transition for the people of Montana. The immigrant families who originally settled the country had either passed away or were at the sunset of their lives. Now the second and third generation children were taking over the major responsibilities for the home ranch and the way things were done changed.

This generation was college educated and they employed modern ranching techniques on their ranches. They used tractors and not horses; they broke up more virgin soil for cash crops laced with new additives; they purchased more land knowing that volume was important for survival; and even the trusted truck was traded for the small four-wheeler that could travel almost anywhere.

This generation also met the land developer, the people who came with cash in their wallets and dreams in their heads. They saw what was happening to the country. People were working less hours, had better means of transportation, had more money to spend, and loved to get away from the crime and impersonalness of the urban life. Montana was ripe for development.

Huge ski areas, fishing villages, hunting camps, golf courses, residential parks and commercial sites were just some of the development that happened. Beautiful ranches were divided into ten and twenty acre plots. But who could blame them? Some ranchers made more money selling their land than they could ever have made ranching full time for many years...and it was a lot less work.

People were even moving into the state without jobs ... wanting to give their families a place to live which was safe and free of urban pollution. However there were many people who moved into the state with secure jobs and skills that brought immediate employment. The coming of the computer age meant that a person could work right out of their home rather than out of a stuffy office on the 21st floor ... and they were willing to pay for the office space.

It was during this time of great transition that the author lived among the people as an adopted son. I was called to serve them as their pastor and friend. I met them, listened to them, cried with them, suffered with them, buried them, and rejoiced with them. I had opportunity to be in their homes and meet some of the people who first settled the area.

I was there when you could go just about anywhere hunting or fishing without worrying about trespassing on private or leased land. Hunting and fishing rights were just starting to be sold by individual ranchers. I was there when the clear trout streams flourished, when cows were moved down the road by horses, and the only piece of blaze orange needed for hunting was still in the store on a bolt of cloth.

The stories which follow cover that span of years. Although they are primarily stories of incidents that happened to me personally, still much of the flavor of those early years in Montana is in the stories. The reader will be able to touch, smell, and feel the excitement of the land which is correctly called, The Big Sky country. It begins with a call...then a place...and finally the stories.

THE CALL

Nearly thirty years ago, my first call out of the seminary was to the great state of Montana. It happened like a football draft system. Graduates from the seminary had their names submitted to the bishops of the church. (The owners.) Then the bishops decided where the seminarian's talents or gifts (how one carried the ball) could best be used for the sake of the whole team.

If one bishop decided that the graduate would work really well on his team (the position on the team is important) then the graduate's name would be shoved to the top of that bishop's list. If no other bishop challenged the first bishop, the name of the graduate was added to that bishop's roster. The name was then given to a congregation by that bishop (one of several teams in that conference) for the settling of the contract.

Even though the bishops assigned you where they felt you were the most needed, still they did give you the opportunity to list three geographic areas of the country where you felt most comfortable serving. (The seminarian with tongue in cheek maintained that it was the bishop's way of saying to the student, "You are important!") The real truth was that it was the need of the church and her bishops that had the final word. But I chanced the system and the Rocky Mountain bishop took notice of my interest.

Having been through the state of Montana a few times prior to my graduation, I knew that it was where this outdoors person wanted to live and raise his family. I liked the country, the mountains, the streams, the plains, and, most importantly, the people I had met. When the members of "my team" sent me letters, pamphlets, and other items of interest, I knew that Montana was where I was being called by the Head of the whole system.

THE PLACE

After my ordination service in my hometown, Pigeon Falls, Wisconsin, my golden retriever dog Major and I headed off for Montana. My wife Mary Ellen and son Mark, and infant daughter Heidi would be flying out to meet me later. My destination was Wilsall (named after Will and Sally Jordan) in Park County. That's where the parsonage was located and one of the two churches that I would be serving. The other church was fifty miles north of Wilsall at White Sulphur Springs.

When I finally entered the state of Montana (driving across North Dakota took awhile), I had my first introduction to Montana. The expanse of the country was unbelievable. Towns like Wibaux, Glendive, and Miles City seemed so far apart that you would have to pack more than a lunch if you were going to visit someone...especially if you were on a horse's back.

It seemed that I had driven forever by the time I arrived in Billings and all I saw were fields of winter wheat...miles of it growing in fields on both sides of the Yellowstone River and unlimited pasture land filled with cattle and antelope. It appeared dry and in need of a good rain...and it was!

When I neared Billings I could see the Pryor Mountains to the south and some of Absarokas off to the southwest. My heart started to beat a bit faster when I saw the snow capped mountains of the Absarokas glistening and dancing in the brightness of the afternoon's sun. I could almost hear them calling out my name.

Proceeding west from Billings, I continued driving alongside the Yellowstone River through towns like Laurel, Park City, Columbus, Reed Point and Big Timber. The closer I came to Big Timber the better I could see the mountains off to the north that would become very familiar to me, the Crazy Mountains. Wilsall was located on the west side of those peaks and White Sulphur Springs was reached by driving parallel to them to the north.

About thirty miles from Big Timber, just a few miles before arriving in Livingston, Highway 87 turns off to the north. I was less than thirty miles from my destination when I made the turn and headed up toward the Shields Valley. Again, a stream, the Shields River, was to lead me right to my doorstep.

Arriving in Wilsall I looked for the church and the parsonage and didn't take long to find it. Wilsall was not one of the most populated places in the world. If everyone was in town at the same time it would probably number about two hundred people. When I drove up to the church and to the parsonage next door to it, I found myself wading in Montana mud (called gumbo) when I got out of my car. I quickly learned the importance of wearing cowboy boots.

The house was small and the best view of the mountains was from the tub in the bathroom. You had to stand in the tub and then peer out to see the magnificent Crazy Mountains off to the east. My wife always made me take off my shoes before getting into the tub...especially after a rainstorm.

The view from the kitchen and living room was a wind swept hill with two or three houses looking down at the parsonage. One of the houses had an outside toilet that had

7

been tipped over. The two holes looked just like a pair of binoculars...and they faced our home.

The parsonage didn't have the luxury of a garage for my car...but neither did anyone else have a garage. When winter arrived (sometimes in July) the tank heater on the car was plugged in every night. There were those nights when it was so cold that not even the tank heater kept the car warm enough to get it started the next morning.

Although the house was small with no garage and a questionable view of the mountains still it was a nice home, comfortable and well maintained by the people, and best of all it was free. That's one of the blessings that some pastors enjoy in their ministry.

This was the place where God called me and and it was beautiful...filled with love and caring. It was where my family got their first exposure to Montana and the place where the stories which follow first started. From Wilsall to White Sulphur Springs, Livingston to Billings, and many of the south central counties of Montana, the stories are remembered.

THE STORIES

John's Hardware Store

Probably the busiest place in Wilsall was Johnny Arthun's Hardware. It was the old fashioned type of hardware store where you could weigh your own nails, smell the leather bridles, and fiddle with some new gimmick on display for a special offer. It was a hardware store where, when you left the store, the children received a lollipop as the parent paid the bill.

It was also the place to go to learn things about the community. The first time I went into the store, John was busy as usual, but he took time to introduce me to several of the local people. I especially recall meeting Mr. Eaton Becker, a big, raw-boned, man who came to Montana from the east and carved out a cattle empire on the Shields. His Herefords were well known around the country as being quality

10

stock.

John introduced me as the new pastor at Shields River Lutheran Church and The American Lutheran Church in White Sulphur Springs. Mr. Becker and I seemed to hit it off together and we talked for a good hour. I learned a great deal about the history of the area during that conversation. Eaton was an active person in the community and seemed to have the pulse well read.

Before he left the store that day, he said, "I realize that you had a long trip to get here, Pastor, and that you probably had some additional expenses along the way. Please accept this as my way of helping." As he was shaking my hand I felt something being placed into the palm of my hand. When I opened it, a twenty dollar bill was in my hand.

I looked at him and said, "Thank you, Mr. Becker, but I cannot accept this gift from you. The congregation in Wilsall and White Sulphur Springs have paid all my expenses. Would you be so kind as to come to church and put this in the offering plate?" His face changed into a look of disappointment and anger. He never said a word to me, but took back the money and walked out of the store.

I learned an important lesson about Montana from that first meeting with Eaton Becker...never refuse their gift. To refuse their gift is like slapping them in the face. It is saying to them, "I don't need you, nor do I need your help!" He never did come to church while I was there.

But I learned other things of importance whenever I visited the store. I learned what common problems were being faced by the ranchers and how they handled them. I learned that it was o.k. to be out irrigating your fields when it was raining...the water got to the roots better. I learned how dependent ranchers were on the weather. Often when they greeted each other they had something about the weather in their greeting.

I also learned that people came to John's Hardware not only to pick up ranch supplies but to get away from the boredom and loneliness of the ranch life. Many came to the store just to get in on some of the latest gossip around the community or to hear a new joke delivered to town by one of the salespeople who called at the store.

People from Montana know how to laugh at themselves and with one another. Jokingly, one person once said to me, "It's the only thing that keeps you sane during the hard winter months." Maybe so, but the Montanans are healthy people because they can laugh and enjoy themselves where they are planted. They never take themselves so seriously that they are not able to adjust to life and move in another direction. It's part of what makes them so special.

But the most important thing I learned at John's Hardware was this...the people take care of one another and love one another, not only in good times, but when pain and suffering invaded their lives. They were very supportive to one another. That message more than any other soon became clear to anyone who met and talked with people on the inside of John's Hardware Store and then paid attention to what happened on the outside.

Testing The Preacher

Everyone in the Shields Valley knew that there was one person who loved being a cowboy more than anyone else...Dick Anderson. He loved everything that went with it...steers, roping, horses, and arenas.

Dick and his wife Marie inherited the ranch from her father and it was a beautiful spread...filled with good grass, water, and buildings. While living there, Dick also built a big outdoor arena for roping and dogging cattle, and it was well used by the local invitees.

Dick was so into the sport that he even purchased longhorn steers from Texas and had them shipped to Wilsall. When they arrived, Dick and his associates drove them up the Shields River road to the ranch. I don't know where they had more fun, in the arena or while driving those cattle up the river road. You could see the old west at work, and for a person who had never seen cattle being driven it was a sight to behold.

Dick also had some of the better horses in the area. In particular, he owned a stud by the name of Keno who was one of most spirited horses around. Keno also had a lot of cow in him and enjoyed arena work. Riding the horse was not something for the beginning student, in fact, some of the more experienced riders avoided Keno.

Well, early in my ministry at Wilsall, our family was invited out to the ranch to watch the roping events. We climbed up on the corral poles and watched the men as they backed their horses in behind the drop cord and waited with rope in hand for the cord to drop and the steer to come

13

bolting out of the chute.

When the cord came down and the chute opened, the horses would bolt out as if shot out of a cannon. The roper would lay the lariat over the steer's head and quickly dally the rope around the saddle horn while the horse set its legs...ready for the big jolt from the weight of the steer. The rope would tighten and the steer would often be laid on its side.

It was fun to watch...but we knew that we were watching a dangerous sport. More than one cowboy has lost a finger dallying the rope on the horn, or suffered broken bones when their saddle didn't hold when the rope tightened.

Then the inevitable happened. Dick rode up to me near the fence and said, "Hey, Rev. (he always called me Rev.), do you want to try it?" I could tell by the way he asked the question, and by the glances of the other men in the arena that this was going to be "testing time" for the preacher. They wanted to see how this preacher was put together. So I looked him straight in the eye and said, "I sure would like to try it."

He grinned and said, "Good, you can ride Keno!" Great, I thought to myself, what have I gotten myself into here. The last time I was challenged like this was when a friend took me to the top of the ski scaffold in Eau Claire, Wisconsin, and said, "Are you up to it?" I flew over 200 feet on the skis that day and now I wondered how many feet I would fly off this spirited horse. But I had made my commitment and there was no turning back.

One thing they didn't know, I wasn't completely ignorant about riding horses, or for that matter, roping cattle. As a child I often rode draft horses around our farm, sometimes with a rope in hand. Our horses didn't have the quickness of saddle horses, but when I was learning how to rope milk cows you didn't need speed anyway, just patience. You would hope that the cows might move.

I climbed down to the arena floor and walked over to Keno...grabbing the reins on his bridle while petting him on the head. I wanted him to know that I was not afraid of him. I slid my foot into the stirrup and lifted myself into the saddle. When I did, he made a few quick jumps to check me out, but I hung in there with him and gave him a shot in the belly to let him know I was going to be in control.

After prancing around the arena for awhile, I backed Keno into the starting gate and made sure the loop was set and that it was held properly in my hand. I can't remember my last thoughts before the steer left the gate, but I'm sure it had something to do with hanging on...and letting the rope slide out of my hand in the direction of the steer.

The cord dropped and Keno shot out of the starting gate as if he had been hit in the behind by an electrical probe stick. The initial lunge was the most exciting...after that he got to his stride and it smoothed out. I waited for a moment or two when we neared the steer and then threw the lariat.

The rope reached out with a large circle and came down in the direction of the steer. It landed on the steer's head, but only caught one horn. Keno was smart enough to know that I hadn't caught the steer so he didn't set his heels. The rope dangled off the steer's head and I knew that I had failed roping my first steer in Montana.

15

Even though I had failed in my first attempt to catch, and hold, a longhorn steer, my willingness to give it a try entered the community pipeline that same day. The word spread that the new preacher had roped a steer at Anderson's, and that he had done it off the back of Keno. I sensed that I had passed an important Montana test...and it felt good.

Fishing the Irrigation Ditch

Having been a fisherman ever since I can remember, I was excited about trying my skills on one of the famous Montana trout streams.   As I traveled to White Sulphur Springs north of Wilsall a couple times each week, I had my eye on several streams that really looked good to me. One was Flathead Creek,   another was Cavanaugh Creek which flowed out of a lake just a few short miles north of town,   still   another was 16 Mile Creek,   and the last one was the South Fork of the Smith River.

There were many other streams and rivers in the area too,   including The Shields River (a brown and cutthroat jewel), Horse Creek, Rock Creek, and Trout Creek.   But I was looking for something near the road where I could fish on my way to and from White Sulphur Springs.   It was a difficult decision, but I finally decided to fish the stream that came out of the lake...Cavanaugh Creek.

When the day finally arrived,   I took my fly rod and headed for the stream.   I had heard that the Woolly Worm was a good wet fly on most streams in the springtime,   so I chose one that looked like a fat caterpillar and slowly waded into one of the pools,   casting the fly ahead of me and letting it settle back into the deep hole.   I did this for nearly an hour without having any success...not even a bump.   I was getting a bit frustrated with Montana fishing.

While I was beating the stream with my woolly worm,   I noticed a pickup truck driving by at a very slow speed.   The driver pushed his hat back and glared out the window in my direction...shaking his head.   I didn't know why he was

17

shaking his head until later.

The vehicle picked up speed and headed south into Wilsall. About a half hour later the truck reappeared along the stream and this time the person spoke to me. He said, "Howdy, I'm Park Swandal, one of Ed Swandal's boys. We live down the road a bit...up on Flathead Creek road. Are you having any luck?" he asked. "No," I quickly answered, "I haven't had even a bite!" "Well," he said with a grin on his face, "maybe you should try fishing somewhere else...you're fishing in an irrigation ditch!"

Now I knew why he shook his head earlier...it was from disbelief. He couldn't believe that I was fishing that ditch. No one ever said anything to my face regarding the incident, but I'm sure that the story covered the area before sundown. My imagination ran wild. I imagined that I could hear the people saying, "That's the new pastor who doesn't know the difference between an irrigation ditch and a real Montana fishing stream, I wonder how he'll do in the pulpit?"

Going To Harlowton

Just beyond Ringling, going north from Wilsall toward White Sulphur Springs, there's another highway heading east which takes you to the small ranching communities called Lennep and Martinsdale. In this area there are some well known Montana ranches: the Bergs, the Grandes, the Bair sisters, the Voldseths, and possibly the most well known of all, the Rankins.

It is a beautiful area, set between the Castle Mountains on the north and the Crazy Mountains to the south. The bunch grass and other native varieties carpet the area, making it a prime area for the raising of beef cattle. But it also can be one of the hardest winter areas in Montana. Snow, cold temperatures, and wind are not uncommon...making the winters downright miserable at times.

I learned this lesson well when some friends invited us to go with them to a pastor's conference in Harlowton, Montana. He was the pastor in Livingston south of Wilsall about thirty miles. The shortest distance to Harlowton for him was through Wilsall. He could proceed north to Ringling, then take the cut- off road through Lennep and Martinsdale to Harlowton. My wife and I accepted his offer...besides, he had a four wheel drive Jeep and it was winter.

It was early Spring and the snow hadn't melted completely from the area. In fact, to the north along the mountains, it appeared as if there might be some weather moving in, but we were unconcerned...we had a four wheel drive Jeep carrying us through the country.

The closer we got to the Lennep turnoff by Ringling, the worse the wind blew...although the sky remained clear and bright. None of us had warm coats with, nor overshoes, caps, or gloves. As we later discovered, we didn't have a sleeping bag, candles, or other items along either. We were not well prepared for what was about to happen.

As we turned east on the Lennep road and traveled about eight or ten miles, suddenly the highway was filled in with a huge drift that extended two hundred yards or more down the road. My fellow pastor put his vehicle in four wheel drive and we made it through...with drifts up over the tires.

Once through the drift, we stopped and breathed a sigh of relief. As we were sitting there, debating about what we should do, a telephone man from White Sulphur Springs met us from the direction we were heading. We asked how the road was behind him and he replied, "Except for a few places, the road is clear." "Just follow the tracks and you should be fine."

With that recommendation we continued on our journey. The repairman was right, we made it through several long drifts as we headed toward Harlowton. But, in a rather remote area west of Lennep, there was yet another long drift looming out in front of us. There were vehicle tracks running into the drift and out the other end, so we nosed the Jeep into the track and cranked the Jeep up to full power.

When we got further into the drift, we realized that it was bigger than it looked, But, at that point, there was no stopping or turning around. Soon the snow was coming up to the hood and the engine area. The engine never failed us, but the vehicle high centered, the snow had piled up under the vehicle so that there was no traction from the wheels. We were stuck...and when you are stuck with a fourwheel drive outfit, you are stuck!

There we were...with little food, inadequate clothing, and no travelers on the road. We got out of the vehicle and looked around. There were tire tracks out on the field next to the highway! What the repairman hadn't told us was that when we came to this drift, rather than trying to drive through it, just go out on the field around it.

We sat in our vehicle with the wind blowing and the cold reaching down into our bones. A decision had to be made. The four of us decided that one man would stay with the women in the vehicle and the other would go for help. We knew that this was not a good safety measure. Safety people tell you that if you get caught like this, stay with your vehicle. That is easier said than done, especially when you are freezing and without food.

I volunteered to go look for help. So, wrapping myself up with what I could find to fight the elements, I stepped outside and headed down the highway toward Lennup. The wind was blowing and the cold was penetrating my flimsy clothing. Not even walking at a brisk pace kept the body from absorbing the cold.

As I was turning a corner in the highway, down to the left of the road was a grey Ford Fergurson tractor parked by a hay stack. I thought to myself, "I used to drive one of those years ago...I wonder if I can get it started?" When I finally made it down to the tractor and jumped into the seat, it came to me how I should start it.

21

A few tugs on the choke, a few clicks on the throttle, and then it was touch the starter time. When I touched it, the tractor growled and groaned but didn't start. So I choked it a couple more times and hit the starter again and it started up. What a sweet sound it was to hear the engine catch and smoothen out. All I can remember saying is, "Thanks, God!"

I backed the tractor away from the haystack and headed toward the road that led to the highway. Once on the highway, I changed gears and moved quickly toward the Jeep. Shortly thereafter, a pickup truck, loaded with armed men, came roaring up to the tractor. The men were waving their arms and yelling at me to pull over to the side of the road. When I pulled the tractor to the side and shut it down, they quickly gathered around it and asked, "What are you doing? Who are you?"

I knew I had some quick explaining to do. When I told them who I was and what had happened, they relaxed and almost started to laugh. From their ranch house they had watched my every move with binoculars. When I drove the tractor up on the road, they got into their pickup, with guns in hand, and came after me.

When the inquiry was over, and everyone relaxed from the tension of the moment, they had me leave the tractor along the side of the road and drove me back to our stuck vehicle. In a few minutes they had freed our vehicle from the snowdrift.

The rest of the trip went well. We arrived at the pastor's meeting several hours late...just in time to have coffee and cake before returning home. Needless to say we took another route back home that evening.

It wasn't long afterwards when I began to hear stories circulating around the whole area about a certain pastor who stole a tractor from a rancher's haystack near Lennep. What I didn't know was that many of those people around Lennep and Martinsdale were related to people in Wilsall and White Sulphur Springs. It is amazing how quickly news travels...especially when the news travels through relatives.

One Watering Hole

Most communities in Montana have their local watering hole...or bar. Martinsdale had one too...and its reputation was well known throughout the country. Let me introduce you to a bit of that reputation. First of all - and it may happen even yet - ranches were won and lost at the poker table at the Martinsdale Bar. Someone would say, "It's just a small game where no one gets hurt, but you might lose your ranch."

Another reputation it had was that it was a good eating establishment...with no dress code. You could see people wearing all kinds of clothes in the place...with western attire definitely having the edge. But at the Martinsdale Bar you could sit down and have one of the best hamburgers in Montana. Not only were they ground from local beef, but the buns were home grown and so were the fries. And it was reasonable.

Still another reputation it had was that it was a place where you could be with people and have some laughs. (Notice I didn't say "some drinks.") Drinks were served there...but it was more than that...it was the atmosphere, the comradeship, and the flavor of the place that kept the people coming.

It was especially busy during hunting season. People would stay in the local hotel or camp with their trailers in the community somewhere during the hunting season and then eat their dinner meal in the Martinsdale Bar. I know...because I ate there myself when elk hunting in the Crazy Mountains.

One evening a friend of mine, Pastor Merv Olson and some other friends had dinner there after a long, difficult, day of hunting in the high country. The place was filled with hunters from the area (called locals) and out-of-staters. Behind the bar they had a new elk bugle on display. (For the novice, an elk bugle is an instrument you normally blow to attract bull elk in the mountains...especially when they are in the rut.) My friend said to me., "Give it a try, Ron, you'll love it."

I should have known better than to pick it up and give it a blast...for my friend was pretty good at setting you up, and besides, people in the bar were watching me pretty closely. But, in one of my weaker moments, I gave it a tremendous blow, and flour which had been packed into it, came roaring out and covered my whole face.

The place erupted and people started coming up to me and patting me on the back. I guess my name is now up on the wall of the Martinsdale Bar. When I blew that elk bugle I joined a host of others...both locally and out-of-state who had their names listed as well.

That's the Martinsdale Bar scene. If you want a good time, especially during hunting season, write it down as one of Montana's finest. But remember, if someone offers you a chance to try out a new elk call, hand it over to someone else before you are as white as snow.

Pizza Express

Montana was not known for its pizza parlors. A good steak, but not pizza. Coming from the midwestern cities of St.Paul/Minneapolis, Minnesota, good pizza parlors could be found every few miles. Not having pizza when you wanted it was one of the more difficult things to adjust to in coming to Montana.

After a couple years, a pretty decent pizza parlor started in the college community of Bozeman and our family visited it frequently...especially after spending the day skiing at Bridger Bowl. But in the beginning, when we first came to Montana, there was no pizza!

In fact, pizza was so new to Montana that I'm not sure if some people even knew what a pepperoni and cheese pizza looked like...to say nothing about how it tasted. But we did, and when we got one of those pizza cravings that set our taste buds to work, we knew something had to be done.

So our family did some creative thinking to get our pizza. A relative from the Twin Cities, Roger Moberg, was a Northwest Airline pilot and regularly flew into Montana. We asked him if he would be willing to bring us pizzas from Carbone's Pizza in the Twin Cities...if Carbone's were willing to package them for us. He agreed to the plan...and so did Carbone's, so thus started the Pizza Express.

The first delivery was within a month. My wife's mother, Elsie Olson, came to Montana for a visit and she hand delivered the first shipment. My cousin, Don Lundberg, from St. Paul, picked up the pizzas and delivered them to my wife's mother at Wold-Chamberlin Field in Minneapolis, Minnesota. She boarded the 727 to Montana, with Roger Moberg as the pilot, with eight partially baked pizzas. The aroma filled the cavity of the plane.

People were excited because they thought they were going to have pizza for one of the "in flight" meals. However, disappointment quickly registered on their faces when they heard the pizzas were being delivered to her daughter and son- in-law in Montana.

When they arrived, we immediately put them in the freezer. Then, whenever we got hungry for a pizza, we would take one out, put it in the oven, bake it until it was done, and celebrate a bit of our place of origin in Montana. We selfishly protected those pizzas as though they were the last pizzas in the world.

The Rodeo

Wilsall and White Sulphur Springs were cowtowns. The biggest event of the year in both places was their rodeo. People would travel from all over the state to be a part of the festivities. In fact, there were several people from outside the state that set their vacation schedules according to the time of the rodeo.

When the time for the rodeo arrived, the towns changed. Horses were hitched up outside buildings, almost everyone wore their western outfits, and there were parties filled with laughter, music, dancing, and drinking. There seemed to be more than just a little of the latter. For example, a friend of mine filled up a pickup box full of beer cans on Sunday morning before church started. He probably could have picked up another load but he didn't want his pickup standing in front of the church loaded down with beer cans.

One year at rodeo time, a relative was visiting our family and he witnessed a rider coming out of the Bank Bar in Wilsall on his horse. The only thing missing was a six shooter blazing away at the moon and stars. He commented, "And I thought the wild west was all gone!" I suggested he walk down main street and count the pickups with guns hanging in back windows and pistols mounted on the steering columns.

So the towns changed at rodeo time, in more ways than just mentioned. The church service was actually well attended. These people always did claim to be church members, it came with their roots. The immigrant Norwegians who settled the country brought with them this respect for the Holiness of God and made sure it was passed down to the children.

No matter how late you got home on Saturday evening, on Sunday you were expected to be in church...especially at rodeo time. No mother (and some fathers) wanted anyone to say that she neglected setting this priority in her family. At rodeo time everyone was watching what everyone else was doing.

It was during my first rodeo worship service that I was introduced to the two Bobs who ushered...Bob Hoyem and Bob Youngberg. Bob Hoyem and his family ranched up the Shields Valley. His parents were still alive when I was there, and they were part of the early group that settled that country. Peder and Tillie Hoyem planted the seeds deeply in Bob and his brother, Arnold.

Bob Youngberg, the other Bob, lived and worked out of Clyde Park, another ranching community a few miles south of Wilsall. Bob's wife and her parents were instrumental in planting the faith in the heart of this man.

Both Bobs were big, strong, and young. They would have fit well into the line of Montana State's football team. Actually, had they been on the line together, I doubt if anyone would have passed their way without experiencing the crunching of body and bone. As I said, they were my ushers on rodeo day.

When the two men came up to the front of the church to receive the offering plates, they had to walk sideways. When they reached out for the small offering plate, their fingers hung over the edge. As I looked up at them at the altar railing I decided right there that I had nothing to fear if these men were on my side, or better, on the Lord's side. No one could snatch those plates out of their hands...who would have dared?

All the calf roping, team roping, or bronc riding was not nearly as exciting as watching the two Bobs coming down the aisle for the offering plates. I always thought the offering was a whole lot better whenever they ushered too.

Horses, A Way of Life

Several years ago most ranchers had a good string of horses on their ranch. The reason was simple...much of the work was done with horses. The popular breeds were: Morgan, Arabian, Appaloosa, and, of course, the most popular...the Quarterhorse.

One of the often heard debates among ranchers was which breed was the best. One was noted for their endurance, another for their working with cattle, while another was noted for easy handling, etc. But, each had their own kind of specialness about them and the problem could never be solved.

My wife wanted a horse, so one of the local ranchers, Derril Arthun, set out to find her one. One day, as he was driving on his land up in Potter Basin, he noticed that someone had abandoned a horse on one of his sections. The horse was without brand and didn't carry any owner papers in his pockets, so Derril loaded him into a trailer and took him to the sheriff's sale in Bozeman.

Derril was thinking about my wife's request when he bought the horse that day. He loaded it back up in his trailer and called Mary Ellen and said, "I've found you a horse...where do you want it?" He paid $75.00 for the gelding and sold it to us for the same price.

What a deal! Our family named the horse, "Old John" because we weren't sure of his age. He was a little wind broke, but he had a lot of cow in him and you could rope off his back. Also, he could cut cows as good as the best and he was quick and smart. He was so gentle that the children could crawl all over him and never put up a fuss, and yet, whenever I got on him and wanted action, he was willing. We had "Old John" in our family for the next 10 years...ultimately dying on the same section where he was first found by Derril.

So, we were in the horse business. I managed to pick up a fairly good saddle (which I still have) in White Sulphur Springs for about $80.00 (more than I paid for the horse). Also, from a rancher in the Clyde Park area, we purchased a homemade two horse trailer for about $250.00. It was a well made trailer, staying with us until we got out of the horse business years later.

Once you have one horse you discover that you need another one...especially with a family that liked to ride. So we added another horse named Starky to our family. He was a registered quarterhorse out of the famous Harold Grafton line. This young, bay colored, gelding was beautiful...with nice conformation, about 15 hands, fast, and smart.

I figured that this horse would be everything I would ever need for work or pleasure, but I was wrong. When I came to pick up the horse I should have given him back to the owner. When I left to get my trailer he was tethered to one side of the corral, when I returned he was on the other side. He had jumped over the wooden fence.

I don't know how he survived that jump because the nylon rope was holding him to the corral post...and it was tied up rather short. When he did it, however, I think he snapped something in his head because when I got him to the new pasture, all he did was keep circling the field inside the fence. It was almost as if the horse had eaten loco weed...but there was none in the field where he was picked up and none in the field where I released him.

Whenever I got on his back, I never knew when he was going to try to dump me. Sometimes he would act as if he was going to break into one of his tantrums and then change his mind. There was no way that a rider could get comfortable on his back because you never knew what he was going to do. Eventually I sold the horse...and our whole family was relieved.

Later, when we moved to Livingston, Montana, just thirty miles south of Wilsall, we found another horse that we purchased from a lady up Mission Creek. It was a mare by the name of Racer and she lived up to that name.

This young thoroughbred/quarterhorse mix was one fast animal. She hated to have any horse ahead of her and would stretch out her legs to make sure that didn't happen. I should have entered her in the horse races at the Yellowstone County Fair, but I never did! In fact she was so fast my son used to chase antelope with her, and on several occasions, he almost got a lariat around one of those prairie goats.

Our family took several trips in the mountains...even before we had Racer. In the beginning Mary Ellen rode Old John with Heidi (age l) on the front of her saddle, and Mark, (age 4) on the back. I would carry all the camping equipment, lunches, saddle bags, etc. on my borrowed horse. As the children grew, one would ride with their mother and the other with me. Eventually the parents stayed home and the kids did all the riding.

33

Montana...as I remember it, are those horses and horse trips to the mountains. I can still hear the children singing and asking questions between bites on their peanut butter sandwiches and hard boiled eggs. And I remember how appreciative we were for the Creator who put the marvel together.

Turning each corner on the trail, God handed us a new present to unwrap and experience....a present which seemed to be more beautiful than the previous. Each new experience was like having a constant supply of Christmas packages delivered with your name on each package. You never knew what you were going to get, but it was sure exciting!

It was a sad day in our household when we lost those horses. Old John died first while on winter pasture in the place where Derrill Arthun first found him and Racer developed a leg problem that could not be cured. Later I sold my horse trailer to a young man with children in Montana. What we have left are some tack, some pictures, and an abundance of fond memories.

Mounted Mountain Pastors

As I said in the article, "Going to Harlowton," the pastors would regularly meet once a month and would bring along their wives and smaller children when possible. Each pastor was expected to host the meeting when it was their turn. In that there were fourteen pastors in our conference, you could expect to host them about once a year.

The conference, like most conferences in Montana, was exceptionally large. It extended from White Sulphur Springs to Roundup, south to Hardin, and back to Bozeman in the west.

It took great commitment to gather at White Sulphur Springs if you were the pastor in Hardin, Montana. The trip was nearly two hundred miles one way.

Of course, in those days, there wasn't a daytime speed limit in Montana. At night the limit was fifty-five mph and if you were picked up exceeding that limit the fine imposed could be rather expensive.

Later they changed the daytime speed limit to sixty five mph, but if you got pulled over by a state trooper you could pay the patrol person five dollars and go on your way rejoicing. Just recently the federal government changed the law again. They decided to allow states to set their own limits. Montana went back to the no daytime speed limit, but they kept the fifty-five limit at night.

One of the first pastoral conferences that my wife and I hosted at Wilsall took place up the Crazy Mountains at a campsite developed by the U.S. Forest Service. The interesting thing is the way we got to our meeting.

My wife and I decided that since we lived in mountainous country, with horses all around, we would arrange horses for everyone who wanted to ride up the U.S. Forest Service trail to the campsite. When we asked some of the local ranchers for their help, they did so willingly.

Two ranchers who were members of my church in Wilsall, Austin Swandal and Howard Keyes, volunteered to be the wranglers for the trip. Although they helped with all the tack and guided us along the way, I had a deeper feeling that they went along just to see if the preachers could ride and survive.

Everyone had a horse except three people. The Lyle Onstads from Bozeman decided to ride up to the campsite in a four-wheel drive (they were a bit older and wiser) and Tom Morgan's wife from Hardin...she was pregnant at the time.

It was a beautiful day and the ride to the campground went without a hitch. Once we arrived, we ate our sack lunches, did some conference business, and had Holy Communion together. After being off the horses for a couple hours, it was harder getting back on them again. Austin Swandal had to help some of them get their feet into the stirrups and then push them to the top of the horse.

The ride out of the mountains went well too, and we didn't lose anyone along the way. One of the pastors, Gene Nielsen from Billings, had a very difficult time walking the next day. I understand that he had a few saddle sores, but he always said that he would do it again.

The Billings Conference became the model for the other conferences in our Rocky Mountain Synod of the old Evangelical Lutheran Church. We always had some different things happening at these monthly meetings and we always had a good time together...even if the ride home was sometimes long and tiring.

Picture That Dude

Many times, while living in Montana, our family would be called upon to help move cattle from winter pasture to summer pasture, and visa versa. This did not happen just at Wilsall, but when we moved to other communities as well. People knew that we enjoyed helping ranchers move their cattle, so they would invite us to participate in this twice a year event.

One rancher's summer range was thirty miles from their wintering ground in Wilsall. His cattle were driven north on Highway 89 from Wilsall to Ringling and then east on a ranching road about four miles toward the Crazy Mountains. It was a test of a cowboy's stamina and patience to trail about four hundred cows with their calves that distance. It wasn't so bad as long as the cows cooperated and the calves didn't tire out and lay down, but, more often than not, that's exactly what would happen.

From one of my elk hides I had the saddlemaker in Livingston fashion a pair of chaps for me. (Elk hides make excellent chaps because of their supple, yet thick, texture.) The saddlemaker put a cross on the bottom of one leg and my initials on the other side. My wife thought the added decorations made them look a little tacky, and they probably were, but I wore them with pride anyway.

When we trailed cattle up the highway, occasionally someone would drive up to us, lean out of their cars with a camera in their hand, and start snapping pictures. More often than not, children would be sitting in the back seat with their windows open, staring at what was around them. Their faces were filled with wonder and amazement. I suspect most of them were vacationers.

I always chuckled when they'd take my picture. Some people would motion for me to ride over near their car and pause while they focused their camera. Then they might say, "Hey, how about a big Montana cowboy smile?"

I never wanted to spoil anyone's vacation by telling them they were taking a picture of a real dude...a pastor from the midwest who may have looked like a native cowboy but didn't have a local bone in his body. In fact, I would play the role, turning my chaps toward them in hopes that someone would ask about the cross, but no one ever did.

I have often wondered what kind of conversation surrounded those pictures after they had been developed. I can almost hear someone saying, "On our way through Montana on vacation, we came upon these ranchers having a cattle drive. Look at that cowboy...and the chaps he's wearing. Is that a brand I see on his one leg?!"

I still have those chaps, but I removed the cross and my initials from the leggings. (Is that an admission that my wife was correct?) The needle marks still show, but they aren't quite as obvious. The only time they are worn now is when my wife wears them to western days at her school. When she wears them, people sometimes take pictures of her dressed in them too. Let's admit it, those Montana chaps just keep on dressing up dudes.

Farming Out a Daughter

Mary Ellen joined me in Montana, with our two small children, Mark (3), and Heidi (1 month), in early April. Those first few months were a busy time for our whole family. We had to get our house settled, learn the names of people in the church and in the community, find a new doctor, dentist, grocery store, and a number of other things that a family must learn when experiencing a new move.

It wasn't easy for my wife because I was away from the family an average of two and a half days a week. I traveled to my other congregation in White Sulphur Springs and stayed overnight on a cot in my office. She had to fend for herself many times, but that's the way it was during those years. Of course, she had a lot of help from the local people, and if it was an emergency, I would drive back.

When winter arrived and the snow turned the mountains white, some of the local women were into skiing...including my secretary, Jerry Arthun. The women would go to Bridger Bowl, near Bozeman, one day during the week and enjoy themselves on the slopes. (Actually it was nearly as close to Clyde Park as it was to Bozeman...going up Brackett Creek road.)

Because the women wanted Mary Ellen to be a part of this weekly activity in the winter, they invited her to join them one day. In fact, the first invitation included both of us. I guess they wanted us to see the mountain and experience the joy and exhilaration of what was ahead. Besides, Bridger Bowl was in its infancy at the time...sporting a rope tow, a T-bar and one chair lift and it was cheap entertainment. Lift tickets were $1.00 per person.

Mary Ellen had done some skiing in the midwest but nothing like Bridger Bowl. I suppose you could have classified her as a beginner to intermediate skier. She was, however, willing to learn and take her chances. As for myself, I had done a considerable amount of skiing...but it was primarily ski jumping, which is a whole different concept. Our skis were about 8 foot long, made of hickory, with three grooves on the bottom, and we shot down a man-made scaffold. You didn't downhill ski with jumping skis.

We accepted the women's invitation, farmed out Heidi for the day, and drove up to Bridger Bowl. It was a beautiful Montana winter day, when the sun glistened and danced on the mountain tops and the temperature hung a little above the freezing mark. Although skiing on rental equipment, with legs that hadn't been used for skiing for awhile, it was a beautiful day...until Mary Ellen and Jerry didn't come off the mountain.

On the very last run of the day, January 15, 1968, the ladies had decided that Mary Ellen had improved enough during the day to go to the top of the mountain. Half way down, in a much easier place than what she had already negotiated, Mary Ellen tumbled and broke her leg...in two places.

By the time she had reached the half way point on that last ride she was exhausted. Although her fall was in a relatively easy part of the hill, her exhaustion probably stressed her body enough to cause injury. She later told me that the longest ride she ever had was that ride down the mountain on the back of a ski patrol person. Normally they used a

41

toboggan to bring injured people down the mountain, but in Mary Ellen's case (because the lifts were closed) she came down on a patrol person's back.

Well, you can imagine what it was like to have a full cast on your leg and a three year old and nine month old to take care of...as well as a husband who was gone part of the week. She was grateful when her mother and father and some other friends drove out from Iowa to pick up some of the slack. But that could not last forever...her parents had other responsibilities to manage. So, we had some big decisions to make rather quickly.

We decided that she could handle Mark and get around well enough with her crutches to do most of the other house work, but there was no way that she could care for a nine month old child. Something had to be done with Heidi.

One of the parishioners volunteered to take Heidi into her home during Mary Ellen's recovery time. When June Miller and her husband Stan picked her up and took her to their ranch, it was not easy to handle. Even though they brought Heidi to the church on weekends and we managed to spend time with her, still she took her first steps at the Miller's and not in her home.

Heidi spent about five weeks at the Miller's ranch, from the last part of January through February. Mary Ellen's mother returned to Wilsall in March, stayed for a month, and then they all went back to Iowa without me. We never did go back skiing with the women that year.

And now, whenever we see the Miller's, they ask, "How is our daughter doing? We'll take her back at any time." One of the Miller boys has said to me, "When you took Heidi back home I felt I lost a sister. I still see her at the table smiling at me as if I were her own brother." That's what happens when you farm a daughter out...and then take her back.

Lutefisk, A Norwegian's Delight

Anyone who has spent any time with the Scandanavians, especially Norwegians, learns very quickly that their holiest of days is the day the church serves its lutefisk supper. Even businesses will close shop early in order that the owner can get to the church and purchase tickets with a low number.

The advantages of getting a lower numbered ticket are several. First, you don't have to wait long to get served. Secondly, the servers give you more fish because the cooks want to know if it is properly cooked. Third, you always get some fish. Sometimes they fail to order enough lutefisk from the Olsen's Fresh Fish Company in Minneapolis, Minnesota. When that happens, the ticket holders with higher numbers sometimes don't get any fish. And, fourth, if you eat early you have more time to enjoy the after effects of lutefisk...which can stay around awhile.

Some people who have married Norwegians, or, in rare cases, Norwegians who have tried lutefisk but can't stand the stuff, have another option...meatballs or ham! Yes, lutefisk is the main dish for the evening (the piece of cod that passes all understanding), but meatballs and ham are offered to those who have not managed to cross the bridge called "tolerance".

But lutefisk or meatballs and ham are not the only things on the menu. Also included are such things as: boiled potatoes with butter poured over them, lefse, cabbage salad, corn, bread, various pies, rummegrut (a flour and milk pudding, served hot with cinnamon and sugar), and a beverage...generally egg coffee.

44

The biggest problem with holding a lutefisk supper in the church is that the smell from cooking the stuff lasts forever. Someone once said that the smell of the fish lingers just long enough for the people to remember the event the following year.

Until my wife arrived in Wilsall the people used the parsonage basement to cook the fish and then they would carry it over to the church basement. She not only dared to wear "mini-skirts" in church (they were really popular in the late '60's), but she also put paste-on flowers on our horse trailer, and then asked the church council not to cook their lutefisk in the parsonage.

Well, it caused a stir in the community, but they knew that this young lady would not tolerate that smell in her house. So they came up with a solution. They built a portable shed outside the back door of the church. From there they had direct access to the basement serving area. They cooked the lutefisk by placing it in a big pot and heating it with a propane torch.

The system worked well and everyone was happy. My wife was happy because her house didn't smell and the men who did the cooking were happy because they didn't have to carry that lutefisk across the parking lot and worry that the starving cats in the neighborhood would attack them.

Most of us have heard about a baseball team that gets into a slump. When the lutefisk supper for the year passes the Norwegians go into a slump! People just aren't themselves anymore. They almost go into a depression. Their heads hang low and they kick the ground...wishing the supper hadn't ended. The good news is that attendance in church increases because they don't want to miss the an-

45

nouncement of the next lutefisk feed.

At Wilsall, John Arthun's brother, Curtiss, would time his fuel run from Livingston to coincide with the end of the lutefisk supper celebration. To cheer you up, with a twinkle in his eye, he would say, "Say, I brought a cold lutefisk sandwich up from Livingston today, do you want it?"

She Paid Cash

I can't remember where I first met her, but once having met her you couldn't forget who she was...she wouldn't let you. Her name was Scotty Prescott and she came to Montana from Wisconsin to buy a ranch. I remember that her father was a warden at one of the prisons back in my home state. When he died, Scotty took her inheritance and headed to White Sulphur Springs, Montana, to fulfill her dream of owning and operating a ranch in Meagher County.

The natives in Meagher County tell the story how she bought her ranch. One day she walked into the bank at White Sulphur Springs and said, "I want to buy a ranch!" She laid a suitcase down on the desk of the bank president and opened it. Inside the suitcase were bundles of money...enough to pay cash for the whole ranch and everything that went with it.

I'm not sure if that's the way it happened, but it made for a good story anyway. It was the story I got, and now the reader's got it. What I do know about Scotty is this, she dressed like a rancher, talked like a rancher, and lived like a rancher.

She wore Levis that were covered with signs of a ranch...and boots that carried the same sign. Her shirt was red plaid and western. Her hair was combed back and there was little makeup on her face. Her hands were weather worn and leathery. She definitely looked like a seasoned rancher.

She also talked like a rancher. I'm not sure if she used

bunk house language, but I talked to her many times about things that ranchers were interested in. Things like: the price of beef, the cost of feed, the price of land, the government allotments, and the latest ranching techniques. Scotty was a very knowledgeable person...but she was also a bit different in the way she lived her life.

One day Scotty stopped by our house to ask me to do something for her. We had visitors at the house from the midwest and she came right into the house, sat down at the breakfast table, and proceeded to eat all the sausages my wife had fried up that morning. Our visitors didn't get a bite.

That was Scotty. When she wanted something, she would move right in and get it. The morning she ate all the sausages, she had something else on her mind besides breakfast. She wanted me to help her get her portable corrals back.

Scotty had loaned the corrals to a person from the Wilsall area. The person she loaned them to was having a feud with a another rancher from the area...over what, I do not know. But the person who borrowed the corrals did something he shouldn't have done. He set them up on the Wilsall person's land without permission.

When the Wilsall person saw those corrals on his property, and discovered who had put them there, he dismantled them, loaded them in the back of his pickup and hid them on his ranch. He knew that it would cause a rumble, but it was his way of getting even with his adversary.

I don't know how Scotty knew that a Wilsall rancher had removed the corrals and hid them on his ranch, but I can probably guess. She knew from talking to people that there were two ranchers from the Wilsall area that were having a feud and that they owned land next door to one another in Potter Basin, the place where they were first set up and then taken down for storage.

When she heard the corrals had been placed on the wrong section by the person she loaned them to, Scotty quickly had it all figured out, and, since I was a pastor in the community, and her friend, I was the logical person to settle the arguments and get her corrals back.

When I inquired about the corrals the rancher gave me a sheepish grin and said, "I'll see what can be done about the situation, but I'll talk only with Scotty about it." The corrals were returned that day, but the feud continued between the two ranchers.

Scotty was appreciative, so appreciative that I was worried that she would stop by our house for breakfast when we had other guests. She never did, but we always looked out the window at breakfast time...especially when we had guests.

A Penny Saved is a Penny Lost

Immediately across the street from Hilda's Restaurant in White Sulphur Springs, Montana, was a bar that wet the whistles of many ranchers in Meagher County. The person who ran the bar was also a trained pastries chef from New York City.

He would walk across the street to Hilda's Restaurant and use her kitchen to prepare some of his delicious and unique pastries and then share them with whomever happened to be around. Of course, all of this was done with the approval of Bill and Hilda Wallin, the owners.

In that I would spend an average of two and a half days each week in White Sulphur Springs, and the Wallin's were members of my congregation, I ate many of my meals in that restaurant. It was while I was having one of her delicious meals that I first met the chef.

He was a huge man, about the same size as Bill Wallin, but younger by several years. He had an eastern accent mixed with a southern drawl...and he was very personable and outgoing. I recall that he always wore a chef's jacket and hat while he was doing his baking. Over the next several months I got to know him fairly well...or so I thought.

One evening, after having eaten my fill of pastries, Bill told me that the chef not only was good at making pastries, but that he was also an avid coin collector...a "professional" is the word he used to describe him. "His expertise is pennies," said Bill, "he's got a bunch of them."

That caught my attention, for I had collected pennies for several years. I probably had some valuable coins among the collection, but I never had them checked by someone who really knew their value. Several people told me that I should have them checked, but I never did. Now, however, I had my chance. I asked the chef if he would do me that favor, and he said he would. So, the following week I brought them to town and turned them over to the expert.

The next couple weeks I was on vacation, so I didn't have opportunity to check to see what he had found. But as soon as I got back, I called him...thinking, of course, that he had found a coin so valuable that it would help me retire early. But when I called him, the chef was no where to be found. In fact, there wasn't even an answer at the bar.

I was pretty concerned when I asked Bill Wallin what happened to the chef...and my coins. He said, "Well, an interesting thing happened while you were away." "What's that?" I asked. "An army of law enforcement officers, and the FBI, came to town with unmarked cars and surrounded the bar...taking the chef into custody," he replied.

He continued, "I guess he was involved with some crime syndicate on the east coast." Then, with a lowered voice, he said, "I guess they took everything in the raid...including your coin collection." I felt sick to my stomach.

I never did get my coin collection back...and I never heard what happened to the chef either. The chef never charged for his pastries, but when everything was shaken out of this experience, I paid a high price for them ...probably more than I would have paid in a bakery back east.

Pheasants at Thelmer's

I first met Thelmer and his wife, Gracie, at a Bible camp meeting at Big Timber, Montana, during the fall of 1967. Thelmer was a big man with a huge smile. You could tell by his firm, and calloused, handshake that here was a man that was accustomed to hard work.

I'm not really sure why, but he and I seemed to hit it off with one another from the very beginning. The bonding we experienced was almost instantaneous. Was it our common farming experience? Was it because we both loved children? Was it because we both loved to laugh and have a good time? I suppose all those things were involved with the bonding...but, whatever it was, it was real and it was the beginning of a long friendship.

During that day we talked on many subjects, but one subject was covered more thoroughly than the others ...pheasant hunting! It started by my asking if he knew where some good pheasant hunting could be had in Montana. Thelmer's eyes suddenly started to shine and he said, "How about my ranch for starters?"

When I listened to him tell stories about pheasants on his property I could not believe it. He told me that he regularly saw fifty to one hundred pheasants on the place many of which walked across his lawn. Below his house, where a small stream meandered to the east, wheat fields, bog grass, cat tails, and alfalfa fields provided cover for some of the best pheasant hunting in Montana.

I looked at Thelmer and said, "Sure...who are you trying to kid, anyway? Only South Dakota has that kind of pheasant hunting...and that was in the 1940's and 1950's." I continued, "I may be a Norwegian, but I'm not stupid."

Thelmer didn't bat an eye and continued, "You have to come over and do some hunting. In fact, why don't you and your family come over for the opening day in October and have dinner with us. The season opens at 12:00, so come a little before noon." I accepted the invitation with little hesitation. Thelmer drew me a map to his farm on a church napkin and said, "Good, we'll be looking for you."

Thelmer's ranch was in Yellowstone County, about a hundred miles east of Wilsall. The closest community, and the address of his ranch, was Broadview, but his ranch was west of that community some miles. It is located in the heart of some of the best wheat growing land in Montana. In fact, the quality of the wheat is so rich in nutrients that it is the only wheat that some foreign markets will buy from the United States.

When our family arrived at the ranch before noon, several pheasants were seen walking along the road and a couple of them flew in front of the car. Needless to say, my adrenalin started flowing and I was ready to hunt. When the Mosdal's asked us to eat before going into the field, I had all I could do to remember that I was their guest.

Being the observant person that he is, Thelmer knew what was going on inside of me. He turned to me and said, "O.K., Ron, why don't you walk down by the pig barn and see if you can spot some pheasants. Gracie has lunch nearly ready, so don't be gone long. We have some other guests for lunch too."

I was elated to hear Thelmer grant me permission to go into the field for awhile before lunch was served. I quickly grabbed my 12 gauge, loaded the chamber with a number six shotgun shell and added some fours to the magazine. I walked down by the pig shed and stepped over the fence into some weeds that were thick and tall.

When I did, I hadn't walked but a few feet when the air exploded with feathers and cackles. There were pheasants flying in every direction. There were so many I didn't know where I should shoot next. Well, to shorten the story, I bagged three roosters in less than a heart beat.

As I walked back to the house, with roosters in hand, I saw Thelmer standing by his door with a smile on his face. He called out to me, "Did you see anything?" I held my roosters in the air and said, "I can't believe it!" Thelmer laughed and said, "Now what are you going to do? You have your limit already. You'll have to spend the rest of the day eating."

At the dinner table that evening, when the other hunters lamented over the fact that they had missed so many birds that day, I was asked to give the blessing. I said, "Lord...regarding the others who hunted here today, give them their meat in due season." My wife groaned, Thelmer laughed, and Gracie keeps telling the story.

Thirty on One Fly

One of my favorite fishing streams in Montana is a creek which flows through Ringling, Montana, called "Sixteen Mile." I was first introduced to the stream by John Arthun from Wilsall. His parents lived along its' banks when John was a youngster. In fact, one of the early homesteads still stands where Billy Creek runs into Sixteen Mile. It's not John's home, but it belonged to his uncle.

Sixteen Mile was not a large stream, probably eight to ten feet in the widest section, but it was deep and cold. It was brook trout heaven. There were some rainbows and natives in the stream, but the primary inhabitants were the elusive brook trout.

When I first fished the stream there were no obstructions on the whole length of the stream...only an occasional beaver pond was formed by the master woodcutter. Later in the 1970s Claude Kiff, a rancher in that area, dug out a five to ten acre earthen pond about half way up the stream, but it was ideally located, not hurting the stream a bit. In fact, it helped it.

John Arthun would often wait at his store for me to come by at closing time. I would bring the coffee, pop, and sandwiches. He provided all the equipment that you'd ever need from his store...plus the bait. We would get to Sixteen Mile about 5:30 p.m. and fish until dark. He would generally go up stream and I would go downstream.

When we returned to the vehicle we would normally have fifteen or twenty brook trout in our baskets. The size ranged from eight to fourteen inches. Occasionally we would catch a brook in the nineteen to twenty inch class. At that time there was no limit to the number of brook trout you could catch and keep. The State of Montana considered them to be a scavenger fish, but we never thought of them that way. We loved to catch them...and loved to eat them.

One Saturday in August, I decided to go up to Sixteen Mile by myself. I decided to try my luck below the spillway at Kiff's dam. I had to work my way down along the bank and then carefully step around a sharp bend in the stream to get into position to use my flyrod.

When I came around the bend, I noticed that trout were feeding on grasshoppers landing on the surface. I reached into my flybox and took out a new Joe's Hopper. After tying it securely to my tippet, I put a good floatant all over it. With the flick of my wrist I settled the fly into the frothy water near the main spill. It just touched the surface when a brook trout grabbed it and scurried about the pool.

Just as quickly as I could, I put the fly back into the water in the same place. Again, before I could even get fully set, a brook trout reached out and had it in his mouth. The frenzie never stopped. By the time I was done with that fly I had caught thirty brook trout. I may have caught the same fish twice, because I did take them off and return them to the water...but there were thirty of them, I counted them.

When I returned to Wilsall that day I spoke to John Arthun about that one fly. His reply was, "Are you sure you didn't take some dynamite with you this morning?" My response was simply, "I did...I brought a Joe's Hopper and it worked like dynamite." He grinned and said, "Maybe we can go back tomorrow after church?" We probably did!

Chico Hot Springs

South of Livingston about thirty miles, near the small community of Emigrant, there is a place that has won the hearts of many Lutheran pastors. The name of the place is Chico Hot Springs. It is a resort and retreat center built close to the Absaroka mountains, just a few miles away from the Yellowstone River.

When I first was introduced to Chico, there was one older building that had sleeping quarters enough for three or four dozen people, a large lobby, and an eating area. They also had a bar in another building that was connected by a walkway, and a building that was used for group sessions behind the sleeping area.

But the most important selling point for Chico was not the accommodations, but the wonderful swimming pool and hot bath that was located on that place. The pool was good sized and at the end of it was a hot tub. The pool was heated by thermal water from the same aquafir as Yellowstone National Park...a few miles to the south, and it was warm. It is the only place in the world where I have been swimming while snow was melting on my face.

This was the site for the annual Rocky Mountain District pastors' retreat. Each year the week after Easter the pastors from within the district, which included Wyoming and Idaho, traveled to this beautiful place for a few days of fellowship with colleagues in the ministry.

Every pastor was expected to be in attendance. It was a mandate from the bishop. About the only excuse for missing the retreat was an emergency...like a death, etc. Even the cost of the event could not be held up as an excuse, for congregations were expected to pay the expenses of their pastor. But few people wanted to miss the event anyway...it was too enjoyable.

However, my first experience at Chico was not that enjoyable. No one really told me what happened at the retreat, nor did anyone tell me how to dress, etc. The information sent out by the bishop's office really didn't say, and I hadn't been in the synod long enough to talk to anyone about it. I was a rookie that had to learn the hard way.

When I packed my bags for the retreat, I packed them with clothes that I had collected for the past several years as a clothing salesman for Rothschild's in Minneapolis, Minnesota. In fact, when I dressed for my initial meeting with the pastors and bishop, I put on a new suit, shirt, and tie. My shoes were shined to perfection and I even washed behind my ears. I thought to myself, "Hey, Ron, you are going to meet some special people today and you better look good...first impressions are important."

Arriving at Chico a bit late for the first group session, I waltzed into the room and could have crawled in a hole. There wasn't a suit or tie in the place. I felt like a duck out of water! I made an impression, that's for sure, but I have never known what kind of an impression. I did overhear someone say, "Who's the dude in the suit?"

Hearing that comment, I made a fast exit to the men's room with my suitcase and emerged dressed like a Montanan... which means, jeans, flannel shirt, boots, and a round, tin box of tobacco in your rear pocket.

Year after year, at the conclusion of the event, there were always some pastors who tried to move the conference to another location, but they had little success because Chico was loved by too many. I never voted to go somewhere else because I would have had to learn how to dress all over again and once is enough.

Shoveling My Way Home

One of my closest friends in Montana, Gene Dreidlein, from White Sulphur Springs once asked me if I wanted to join him on a horse trip into the Crazy Mountains. He wanted to go up to Crazy Lake and do some camping and fishing. It must have been one of my weaker moments for I accepted his invitation.

To get to Crazy Lake was no easy matter, for it was accessible only during the summer months. It is located over the top of Crazy Peak (10,000 feet) and down the other side about 2,000 feet. One slip of your horse, or misplaced footstep, spelled instant obituary column.

From the top of the mountain the beauty of the place is almost impossible to describe. Looking back in the direction from which we came, you could see the Absaroka Mountains to the south, the entire Shields valley from Livingston to White Sulphur Springs, the Big Belts to the west, and the Castle Mountains to the north.

Looking east in the direction of the lake you could see from Big Timber, in the south, to Harlowton, in the north. You could see the other peaks and valleys of the Crazy Mountains and the view of Crazy Lake from the top was indescribably beautiful. We even saw some mountain goats grazing on one of the distant peaks.

We arrived at our campsite late in the afternoon. The first thing we did was to set up our tent...making sure that it was well secured to the ground. The winds can get very vicious in the mountains, and the rain is cold.

The next thing we did was to take care of our transportation...the horses. They had to be fed and given water to drink. Once that was completed, we would string a lariat between two trees and tie them to it with their halter ropes. The lariat was strung about shoulder high on the horse in order that they could pass back and forth under it during the night.

Before packing it in for the night, we took our rods and went down to the lake for the evening fishing...hoping that we would catch some fish for dinner. The fish had other ideas... we didn't catch any. We did, however, see something strange. Along the bank of the lake there was a dead deer. It was partially in the water.

Then we saw some dead fish along the lake as well. No wonder we weren't catching any fish...something had polluted the lake. We hesitated taking any of the water from the lake into our camp for cooking that evening. Instead, we climbed up the mountain to a little spring that was flowing down toward the lake and filled our buckets with running water.

While we were cooking our dinner, we noticed that it was getting colder and then it started to rain. Even that early in the night we noticed that the rain was showing signs of turning into snow. We didn't like what was happening, but we were there for the night, so we decided to retire early and wait for the morning.

When we woke up in the morning to a bright sun we saw a whole new world around us. Snow covered the ground where we camped, and the mountain we crossed to get to this place was covered with white crystals. In fact, you could not make out the trail on the side of the mountain.

Both of us had this gnawing feeling in our stomachs that we were stuck in this place...with little food, horses to tend, and bodies to keep warm. The worst part was that the weather looked like it could change again.   There were clouds to the north that didn't look friendly. We knew that we had to get out of there before another storm set in.

After talking at length about our limited options, we decided to take our chances by finding the trail and riding the horses until the trail could no longer be seen. At that point we would dismount and lead them out.   Once having agreed on the plan, we quickly broke camp, mounted the horses, and set out for the top of the mountain.

The trail was easier to find near the bottom half of the mountain, but the more we got near the top, the less one could see the trail.   When it came time to dismount and lead the horses you had to get off on the wrong side or else you might slip and slide down the mountain. When the time came to dismount, I was probably as careful as I have ever been in my life, for the trail could not be seen by the naked eye. Finally, I sat down and told Gene that to go any further would be very dangerous and life threatening.   We needed a shovel and we didn't have one.

As I sat there, wondering what to do, I felt something unusual under my seat. I resettled my body to another spot and dug away the snow that was covering the object.   It was a piece of board, about four foot in length and four inches wide. I never noticed it when we crossed the mountain the previous day, but now...here it was!

When Gene saw it he said, "Now I know why I asked

this minister to go with me!"   When we shoveled our way over that mountain and finally put the horses into the trailer on the homeward side, I said to Gene, "Yup, we had extra help today."   I continued, "Probably one of the first things that I'm thinking about buying is a shovel...how about you?"

Hunting in Paradise

When I received my first call from the seminary, to serve congregations in Park and Meagher Counties, the people sent me a colorful brochure promoting the area where I would be living. In the brochure there were pictures of monstrous elk and deer in their native habitat, and beautiful streams meandering through mountain meadows lush with green grass and flowers. The brochure did what it was supposed to do...it sold me on the country.

I could barely wait to get "on board" in Montana. I believe that my whole life had been spent preparing for it. I felt prepared for my work of ministry, but there was one preparation that still needed my attention. I needed a rifle. That was solved at my ordination.

At my ordination service I was given gifts of money from the special guests. I confess that I didn't use the money to purchase some ecclesiastical garb, but a Winchester, Model 70, 270 caliber rifle...complete with a Weaver 3X9 variable scope. It was one of the new models with a floating barrel...which I later embedded with fiberglass for better accuracy.

The brochure was accurate in describing the amount of game in the area. One evening our family drove up one of the valley roads leading to the Crazy Mountains and counted over 400 deer in just a few miles. There were so many that the Montana Fish and Game allowed each person with a license two deer each season. They could either be both bucks or does, or a combination of both.

There were also large herds of elk roaming the mountains, especially around White Sulphur Springs. Elk didn't get established in the Crazy Mountains until the early 1970's. They migrated across the Lennep flats from the Castle Mountains. Today the herd in the Crazies is probably larger than the herd in the host mountain, but when I first came to Montana, the Crazy Mountains had few elk.

There are numerous stories that could be shared regarding hunting elk and deer in paradise, but a couple stand out as special. We had lived in Wilsall for a couple years when my son Mark suddenly figured he was old enough to go deer hunting with his father. (Actually, he couldn't have been much over five or six at the time.)

I told him that we would go the next weekend..on Saturday. When Saturday arrived, we headed up Shield's River road...watching the fields near the creek when suddenly I saw a large herd of deer on the edge of the field. I pulled my vehicle over onto the field and glassed the herd. I saw a big buck in the group that deserved more of my attention, so I put my scope on his front shoulder, took a deep breath, and started to squeeze the trigger.

Just as I was about to unload the chamber, Mark called out and said, "Dad, Dad, look over there." He pointed toward the hill overlooking the road. He had spotted a buck that made mine look like a yearling. The huge buck turned and started moving away. I took careful aim and sent the bullet accurately to the mark. He died before touching the ground.

We were back home before 8:30 that morning, with a buck that weighed over 200 pounds. The horns weren't that massive, but there were five points on each side and balanced perfectly. The story is remembered and shared not

67

so much because of the size of the buck, but because my son Mark had spotted it for me. I knew he would be a hunter too!

The other deer story happened while hunting with the postmaster from Wilsall in the Castle Mountains. We were driving down an old logging road in the woods when we first saw the magnificent animal. He jumped across the logging road in front of our vehicle, stopped on the other side, and looked directly at us. His rack was so huge I thought at first it was a bull elk. The rack had to have measured over thirty inches.

I quickly pulled the vehicle over, grabbed the door handle, opened it, and jumped out with my rifle in hand. I cranked a bullet into the chamber, took quick aim, and pulled the trigger. The buck went down on its front knees, paused for a moment, and then shot forward like an exploding missile into the woods. I yanked the keys out of my truck, grabbed my backpack and headed after the wounded animal. That's where we made a mistake...we should have let him go and lay down...but we were too excited.

Several times that morning we saw where he had lain down in a bed of snow, but whenever we got near him the only things we saw were the bed, the tracks and the blood on the snow. He was out of there before we could get another look at him.

On two occasions that day we got a quick view of him, but I couldn't shoot because my partner was in the line of fire the first time, and the second time the trees filled my scope. Finally, by 4:00 p.m. we had tracked him to the woods edge...near a larger logging road. But with one giant leap he soared over the road and landed on the other side where the timber was even thicker. When that happened we gave up trying to find him...we were too tired and it was late.

That animal lived to talk about his day in the woods with his fellow deer friends...and I salute his determination. Obviously his wound was not fatal and I was glad. I do not believe in leaving wounded animals in the woods. Of course, I would have appreciated having that rack on my wall, but that's the excitement of hunting...you aren't always successful, sometimes the animal wins.

You are even less apt to win hunting elk. They are the giants of the mountain...and the ghosts, so called because of their ability to disappear. Even yet, as many years I have associated with elk, I cannot get over the fact that such a large animal can be as quiet as a mouse in the woods...even when they are running.

They lay their massive horns back on their bodies and silently move through some of the heaviest dog hair timber like a cat on the prowl. Their lungs, too, have such great air capacity that they can run straight up a mountain and cover many miles in a few minutes. What an animal...and what a challenge to hunt. If you are fortunate enough to harvest one, you not only have a prized animal but some very tasty eating as well.

Again, like deer hunting, there are many stories about elk hunting that deserve to be told. Let me begin by sharing what an old and very successful elk hunter once told me. He said, "If you want to hunt elk, the best time to go is when the weather is foul and the wind is blowing your hat off."

The wind was howling and the snow had been piling up all day when I got my first bull elk. It was just a spike bull, but it was a bull...and I stalked him while he was taking an afternoon snooze. There were larger bulls in the group, but I remembered the advice of another successful hunter. He said, "If you see a bull, especially in the woods, better take him while you see him, because if you take your eyes off him and look around, sometimes you can't find him back."

In other words, don't let your opportunity get away. You seldom get a second chance with an elk. I rejoiced as much over the spike bull as if it would have had five points on each side. It was my first bull...but not my last.

The first really big bull I saw was when my brother Conrad came to Montana to hunt with me. He saw the animal first and pointed it out to me as I was coming down the mountain toward him. I was a thousand yards from where he was standing when he started shouting and frantically pointed his hand up the mountain.

When I walked out closer to the edge of the woods and looked back, I saw what was making him shout. A herd of elk had moved out on a park above me, a half mile away. In the middle of the herd stood the biggest bull I have ever seen in the wild in our country. In fact, I have only seen two bull elk similar in size to Mr. Majestic, one tame bull in Aspen Park, Colorado, and the other in Outer-Mongolia.

There was no way that I could have climbed back up to the park in time to shoot before closing hours. I just stood there with my scope on the animal and fantasized about having that bull within reach of my rifle. At that time I also named him Mr. Majestic and made a vow to myself that I

70

would concentrate all my hunting hours to finding that bull.

The following year I went back into that area looking for Mr. Majestic. The entire morning of the hunt I combed the area carefully with my binoculars and never saw an elk's hair. I did see some tracks, but nothing stirred as I paced up the mountain toward the top. When I neared the top of the mountain I was tired and hungry so decided to take a break.

I picked out a big stump that had a view of the mountain from three sides. At my back was a growth of timber that looked like dog hair...thick and close together. Just as I sat down and opened my backpack, I heard the rustling of trees behind me and an elk grunt. It totally surpised me.

When I managed to get through the thick pines, with my rifle used as a plow, all I saw was the back end of Mr. Majestic going into the woods below me. I stood there kicking myself and in awe over the size of his leaps. I walked down and measured some of the leaps. They measured between twenty and thirty feet. The earth was completely chewed up where his big hooves landed. That was the last I saw of him that year.

That winter I happened to overhear a person talking to a friend about a recent flight he made over the Crazy Mountains. He came upon this herd of elk in their winter range and flew down for a closer look. He told the other person that there was a bull elk in that herd that dwarfed everyone else. He was either a seven or an eight point elk. I spoke up and said, "I know that elk, his name is Mr. Majestic."

The following year I had my final look at Mr. Majestic, the Crazy Mountain ghost. Our party had hunted hard for a week and did well. Charlie got a bull on Monday, I missed one on Wednesday, and Robin got his on Friday. Saturday morning, the last day of our hunt, we were exhausted and decided to sleep in. That didn't last long...the thought of possibly seeing Mr. Majestic got us out of bed about a half hour late.

We parked our vehicle in our usual place and Robin went up the mountain on one side of the valley and I on the other side...as was our custom. When we arrived at the top we would then decide what area to hunt on the way back to our vehicle.

We had barely left one another when Robin started shooting. I ran to a clearing and looked up toward the top of the mountain. About six hundred yards above me, in a park surrounded by trees on two sides, seven bulls were counted milling about the park...confused from not knowing where the shooting was coming from.

I brought my scope up, picked out one of them with a heavy rack, held my breath, and squeezed the trigger. The bull never moved...he just stood there. I quickly brought another shell into the chamber and shot again. By the time I repeated the action several more times, my rifle was empty. But the elk still stood in the same place.

Finally, after what seemed to be an eternity, I decided to step back, reload, and move up the mountain toward the bull. Using the trees for cover, I moved quickly toward the open park. After covering nearly three hundred yards, I regained my breath behind a boulder. After a few moments, I leaned against the boulder and moved slowly around it. Soon the park was in view...and the elk too. He was still there. I rested the gun on the boulder and touch off a shot that crashed into his front shoulder. This time he went down for good.

After a few moments I heard Robin yell, "Did you get him?" "Yes," I hollered back. "Great," was his response, "it's about time." When Robin came up the drainage toward me he said, "Didn't you see Mr. Majestic," he asked? "No," I answered, "I never saw him." All I heard next was the word, "Rats!"

The rest of the story is this. My first shot caught the three point bull in the front foot. All my other shots had been hitting the snow around him, but the first shot got him in the foot and he didn't want to move. After I had run up the mountain for a better shot at the wounded bull, Mr. Majestic walked around behind me. Had I turned around I would have probably seen him. That's what Robin was shooting at, but he missed too!

The final story about elk hunting (although I could tell several more) also happened in the Crazy Mountains. It happened after a big snow in middle November. The weather report promised that the snow would let up, but that there would still be some clouds hanging low in the mountains. I decided it would be a good time to go elk hunting...even though I didn't have anyone to go with me. (That is not a very smart thing to do.)

As I climbed up the mountain, suddenly I got out of the clouds and the view was unbelieveably beautiful. There was a pink hue over the top of the cloud cover, brought on by the rising sun. Here and there you could see the larger peaks of the Crazies and Absarokas sticking their faces up above the clouds like a child poking its head out of the covers.

I sat down to take in the peace and tranquility of the view, when shortly I heard the sound of a dog barking. I thought to myself, "Who is up here with a dog?" Just then, in the same direction as the barking sound, I saw something move on the skyline. Soon an elk's head appeared...then another, and another. All total there were eight elk coming right toward me. They were all cows and calves.

Soon they were right below me. I could have jumped on the back of one of the cows. They never knew I was there. Their keen sense of smell told them that something was different about the place, but my motionless body and quiet breathing left me undetected.

I wondered where the bulls were and why they weren't following the cows and calves. I strained my neck very slowly to the side and eyeballed the openings around me. There they were...two of them, cutting across the parks to my left. I knew that if I were to get them I would have to move up the mountain very quickly.

When I moved, the cows and calves below me went almost beserk. One cow jumped up in the air, passed air, and headed back in the same direction from which it came. The others went beyond me into the woods. I quickly rose to my feet and started up the mountain. I was too late. The bulls crossed ahead of me and ran down the mountain on the other side. Again, I didn't get a bull, but I got the thrill of seeing them and being in that beautiful country. That's worth the price of admission.

I have had numerous opportunities to harvest a nice bull, but it didn't happen until I had left the state and returned as a non-resident hunter. I had shot two or three spikes, a three point, and some cows, but I never harvested a six point until I returned as a visitor. Since that time, I also harvested a big bull in Outer-Mongolia. That six point is on my office wall.

So, hunting in paradise brings great rewards for that person who is inclined to spend their days climbing in high places, eating cold sandwiches, and sipping hot coffee out of a thermos carried in a backpack. Hunting in Montana is worth every twig scratch, every fall on slide rock, every grunt from pulling out elk meat, and every comment from an understanding wife. I'll do it again, just you wait!

Funerals are Dangerous

There are many stories that can be told regarding funerals in Montana. For instance, one of my clergy friends was performing a funeral in his church when suddenly without warning, a person came running up the aisle to the casket. The person paused for a moment, gave a huge groan, then grabbed the deceased and lifted the body out of the casket.

The person would not let go of the body. He defied anyone who attempted to take it away from him. Finally, after some time, a close friend managed to calm him down and returned the body to the casket. The funeral continued without further disruption.

On another occasion, I was called to officiate at a funeral of a ranch hand who had died while herding sheep in the mountains. When I arrived at the mortuary I noticed that no one else was around. I wondered whether I had written down the wrong date and time for the funeral...but I had everything right.

Talking to the mortician I said, "Am I here at the right time?" He replied, "Yes, and the service will start promptly at 10 a.m., as scheduled." When I walked into the chapel there were only six people seated up front...the pallbearers. No other people attended. It was one of the saddest funerals I ever attended.

On another funeral occasion, I had a rather interesting selection of songs played and sung. (This was prior to my getting educated by my associates on the subject.) The songs selected were, "To Dream the Impossible Dream" and "Empty Saddles." It was difficult preaching with the words of those songs still lingering in my mind. They weren't songs recommended by our liturgical commission.

Two of the most humorous things that happened at funerals in Montana were the time when a person slipped on the snow and slid part way into the gravesite, and secondly when a preacher was shot by the honor guard. Let me begin with the first story.

The snow had fallen for the first time that year and the ground around the gravesite was wet and slippery. As the pallbearers carried the casket to the platform that lowers the casket into the grave, one person lost his footing and barely escaped sliding into the opening.

But later, when a person from the lodge was giving a final eulogy by the casket, things did not go as well. The person's foot slipped out from under him and down he went...into the hole. Even though the funeral director and his staff acted quickly to pull him out, I noticed the smiles of the irreverent, including my own.

But the funniest thing happened at a gravesite in White Sulphur Springs to one of my predecessors. He was conducting a graveside service for a veteran when he felt a sting on his torso and noticed blood seeping through his clergy shirt. He had been accidentally (we think) shot by one of the honor guards assigned to the detail.

As the guards were shooting their volleys in honor of the deceased, one of the guards did not get his rifle all the way up to his shoulder in time to synchronize his shot with the other members of the squad. In his haste, he pulled the trigger while coming up with his rifle...and the tip of the blank came shooting out of the barrel, hitting the preacher in the chest.

He was o.k., but he lost some blood. Later I wrote him a letter promoting a new line of clergy shirts. I called the shirt line "Clergy Protect." The shirts were guaranteed to be bullet proof and they came in all liturgical colors. He never ordered one...I wonder why not?

Yes, funerals can be dangerous in Montana.   My suggestions for anyone who attends one is this...stay awake, watch out for snow, and keep an eye on the honor guard.

His Name Was Major

Many people have said these words to me, "I once owned a beautiful dog and after it died I could never find another one like it." I share those same thoughts. Several years before moving to Montana, we purchased a registered golden retreiver to celebrate the birth of my son, Mark. We named him, Major, to go with his golden color.

At full growth, Major weighed about seventy five pounds and sported a deep reddish color to go with his intelligent looking face. Even before he was six months old he knew the basic commands: sit, stay, heel, lay down, and retrieve.

I had classes at the seminary in the morning and in the afternoon I studied...going to work in a clothing store later in the day. But, around 3:00 p.m. each day, I would take a break from the books and bring Major with me down to a lake near our house. I would throw dummies into the water for Major to retrieve. We started with one dummy and ended up with several. He seldom missed any of them.

At the same time I purchased a duck from one of the local farmers and taped its wings so it couldn't fly. I would plant the duck either on ground or in the water and then send the dog out to get it. Even though I kept him from seeing where I had planted the duck, Major would retrieve the duck by watching my hand signals.

Major not only turned out to be a great hunting dog, but he was a close friend, companion to our whole family, and watch dog. In fact when I served a church in Angle Inlet, Minnesota one summer, Major kept watch over my son near the water.   If he got too close to the water Major would get between the two...protecting him from any tragedy in the water.

When the fall of the year arrived and the trees started to take on their fall colors, Major would start to get excited. He loved to hunt, and he was good at it.   Once, while hunting pheasants with a friend, he wounded a bird and it landed on an island that we could not access.   My friend told me to call back my dog...nothing could find that bird. But Major found it. He swam across the water to the island and emerged a half hour later with the rooster in his mouth. My friend said, "If I wouldn't have seen it, I would never have believed it."

Major made several retrieves during his life that amazed many people...including myself.   Once, while hunting ducks with Henry Questad from Livingston three ducks were downed as they came over our decoys.   One landed close to the shore, another toward the middle of the lake, and the third duck dropped across the lake, dove to the bottom and drowned hanging onto a weed.

Major retrieved all three of those ducks...including the third one. He swam across that lake, looked down in the water until the duck was seen, and then dove down and got it in his mouth.   Again, Mr. Questad said, "I would never have believed it, if I hadn't seen it with my own eyes...what a phenomenal dog!"

A few years later Major made another sensational re-trieve.   Henry and my son Mark were along and watched the drama unfold. (Actually, that's all Henry could do that day was watch because he forgot to get his duck stamp.) It was also the day that Henry set his alarm for 2:00 a.m., rather than 4:00 a.m.

He got up, dressed, took his dog for a walk, had breakfast, made his sandwiches, and then waited for me to show
up. When I didn't show, he looked at his watch and discovered why I wasn't there yet. His embarrassment showed
when he told me what had happened.

But Henry got to witness the retrieve that Major would
make that day. The morning hunt was relatively unsucces-
ful, so we decided to head for home. Mark was already in
the back of the Scout with Major and I was putting away
the decoys. Henry was unloading my gun for me and accidently jammed a shell between the chamber and magazine.
He was trying to shake it loose but it was stuck.

Just then I heard the sound of geese honking and coming
in our direction. I turned toward the sound and the three
honkers were coming into the lake right behind my vehicle.
They were so close that I could see the movement of their
eyes. I yelled for my shotgun and Henry quickly gave it to
me. "It's jammed," he said, pointing to the shell stuck between the chamber and the magazine.

Knowing the shotgun as I did, I quickly unjammed
it and drove a shell into the chamber. Spinning quickly to
my right, I managed to get a shot off at the trailing goose.
The goose shook from the impact of the lead hitting its
body, but it did not fall. It continued flying toward the
lake, but then it happened, the goose fell into the water.

Major was watching the drama from the back seat of the
vehicle. The minute I shot Major jumped out of the Scout
and headed toward the downed goose. I was a bit nervous
because a live goose can take the eyes out of a dog with one

strike from their bill. But Major never hesitated. He dove off the embankment, swam out to that live goose and grabbed it. He turned and headed back toward me with that large honker in his mouth.

When he got to shore and started coming back toward the vehicle, my son, Mark, called out his name. Confused by the change of voice, he dropped it. The goose immediately ran and partially flew back into the lake. This time it was more toward the middle of the lake.

Major ran to the edge of the lake, dove off the embankment and swam out to the goose a second time. He grabbed the goose by the neck and dragged it back to shore. Once back on shore, he readjusted his grip on the goose and brought it right up to me...wagging his tail behind him. The goose was still alive, but not for long.

Major was with us for many years. One day in Billings, I was working in my office when Mary Ellen called me with the bad news. Major was losing his hearing and had crossed the street in front of our house. As he was crossing, a pickup truck came by, speeded up, and hit him. The person never even stopped to offer his help,

When, between her sobs, she said that Major had been killed, I almost died myself. Tears were streaming down my face as I quickly drove home to be with our friend. When I buried Major in the backyard, and placed a cross over his grave, the tears continued. We had lost a great friend and a great companion to our family.

Since that time we have had several great golden retriever dogs, but none of them have ever compared with Major. He was truly a phenomenal dog in many ways. The good news is that I believe someday we will see each other again. When I do see him again, my first statement will be, "Do you want to go hunting?" I can see his tail wagging already!

Breakfast With Dad

I suppose every father has something special that they enjoy doing with their children...something that bonds them together. Some fathers may take their children skiing, others may go shopping with them, or go out for ice cream ...the possibilities are endless. In our family the bonding occured around a breakfast table in some local restaurant.

The tradition started when I became the pastor of the American Lutheran Church in Livingston.   Each Sunday one of my children would rise before 6:30 a.m., dress themselves, and be prepared to go to breakfast with Dad. Afterwards, we would go to church where I would work on my sermon and they would do homework, read, or practice their piano.

At one of the breakfasts (in the Murray Hotel) in Livingston, I still recall when my son ordered liver & onions. It created quite a stir among the natives. Not many people order liver and onions for breakfast, especially at seven or eight years of age.

Breakfast conversations would vary...school, friends, family, future plans, joys and sorrows, hurts and disappointments, and questions about life itself.   Subject matter was not nearly as important as just being together.   In fact, it didn't really matter if anything great or earth shaking came out of the meeting, it was our way of saying to one another, "I love you and care about you."   It was our time for bonding.

The breakfast meetings were so important for both children that if they missed their turn, there was no making it up the next Sunday...they made sure of that!   In fact, whenever one of them was away from home, and the other could go with dad two times in a row...or more, that was even more special.

Even now, after the passing of many years, the children still talk about those breakfast meetings with their father and how those meetings provided them with a non-threatening arena to ask complicated and complex questions about life.   As for myself, I really got to know my children, and I learned many things from them in return...things that often filled in as illustration in my morning sermon.

I'm not sure if those breakfast meetings would have ever happened if we had lived somewhere else other than Livingston.   The community had great restaurants...and from our home we passed right by them to the church.   I never could resist good food...and neither could my children.

Bertha Heads to New York

The church in Livingston owned their own bus...a school bus that held about thirty eight passengers. The youth of that congregation named the bus Bertha. When I became pastor of the church the bus had already been driven many miles, mostly to transport youth to the Christikon Bible Camp...a real ten mph trip in the mountains south of Big Timber fifty miles.

The bus, despite the bone shattering trip up to that bible camp several times each summer, was a great machine and gave great service year after year. Of course, there were people in the congregation who maintained it and kept most of the bolts and nuts from falling off.

One year the youth decided to put Bertha to her biggest test...a trip to New York City. A Lutheran youth gathering was scheduled at Madison Square Garden for over twenty five thousand people from around the world, and our youth wanted to attend. Bertha was called on to get them there and back.

The trip was going to be over four thousand miles...at a maximum speed of fifty mph, if a wind was at your back. The bus had no air conditioning and the seats were hard from the beating they received on the bible camp trip. Most of the windows could be opened, but there was no guarantee that you could get them closed again. But, Bertha was a good runner. She used no oil and averaged about twelve miles per gallon on the highway.

When the day arrived to leave for New York, fifteen youth and three adult sponsors, along with their luggage, guitars, food, and sodas boarded Bertha. On the side of the bus they attached a sign which told the world where they were heading...New York City! Soon after departing Livingston, one of the youth, Steve Kramer, started playing his guitar and leading the group in the song, "Cecilia." If that song was heard once during the trip, it was heard a hundred times.

The first few days went fairly well. Everyone seemed to be enjoying the novelty of the idea and they didn't even mind the inconveniences of traveling on a hot bus. We had made prior arrangements to stay at individual churches along the way, so we always had a roof over our heads.

The churches would provide us an evening meal, a place on the floor to sleep, and the use of their facilities. We would make our own breakfast and prepare sandwiches for the day of travel. In appreciation for this, the youth did a service in the evening for the youth of that church. They were often the highlight of the trip.

The first real test came the day we left Luther College in Decorah, Iowa. We loaded the bus early, as we had a long way to go that day. Decorah is located in the hill country of eastern Iowa and those hills, for a bus, can become a real challenge.

As I pushed, shoved, and prayed for the bus to get over those hills, I had moments wondering if Bertha could handle any larger hills ahead.. I was relieved when we made it to the top. I knew, then, that we would make it over the higher mountains to the east.

Soon, however, my enthusiasm changed. The bus lost a clutch coming up those high hills. Fortunately, I had just shifted the bus into fourth gear and was able to drive it to the next town, Waukon, Iowa, twenty miles down the road without any difficulty. When the turnoff came, I braked Bertha and headed into town...stopping completely at the first four-way stop sign near the city center.

I opened the door and stepped out of the bus. As I did, a person passing by said, "Are you having some trouble?" When I explained who I was, where I was going, and what my cargo included, he said, "Wait here." In a few minutes he returned with two other men...both mechanics. Within less than two hours time they replaced our clutch and we were back on the road again. We had no further mechanical difficulties all the way to New Jersey.

Arriving in New Jersey, we parked Bertha at a church close to New York City. Then we took public transportation into the city the following day. The closer we came to the inner city, the quieter the youth became. They had never seen anything like it in their lives. People were everywhere and the buildings reached to the sky...scraping them like one of our Montana mountains.

Our hotel was near Madison Square Garden, making access to the events fairly simple. What was not simple was getting to our rooms. The hundreds of youth in the hotel would punch every button on the elevator. Sometimes you had to wait a long time to get on the elevator, and when you finally did get on, the elevator would stop on every floor. Some people gave up waiting and walked up the stairs.

The New York event was well worth all the hassles in the hotel. When the youth said their farewell's to all the new friends they had met from around the world, it was even quieter going back to Bertha in New Jersey.

Bertha was waiting for us...rested and ready for the trip back to Montana. However, as I turned on the ignition, she refused to start. Bertha had rested so much that she had let her batteries run way down. Again, a couple of people were there to jump start Bertha and we were on our way home.

Just as we were about to leave New Jersey, Bertha started to sputter and miss. I quickly pulled off the freeway at the nearest filling station...not knowing a soul in the place. Again, as before, a guardian angel was watching over us. The man was an ex-schoolbus driver...and had driven a bus just like Bertha.

When I told him that I had trouble with the battery earlier, he said, "Did you know that the battery in this bus is a negative ground system?" I said, "It's the first I had ever heard of that." He took the battery out and recharged it correctly. He put the battery back in place, turned on the ignition, and Bertha never sounded better.

We were gone just over twenty days on the trip, and when we crossed the border back into Montana the youth burst out with the Montana state song...singing it like I had never heard it sung before. They were glad to be home...but happy to have had the experience that would be with them the rest of their lives.

The guitarist and "Cecilia" singer, Steve Kramer, later became a pastor. Steve said the trip to New York City played an important role in his decision to enter the ministry. As for Bertha, she was not retired, although she certainly deserved retirement after that trip. I was called to

89

another ministry, in another city, Billings, shortly thereafter. The last I heard was that she was still making runs
to the bible camp...helping out wherever she could.

Heavy Winds

They have a saying in Montana, "If you don't like the weather, stick around five minutes." They also have a saying about the wind in Montana. "If you board a bus in Billings and head west, when the bus gets to Big Timber, and you step off, you blow away. When you exit the bus in Livingston, the bus blows away.

Winds can be pretty awesome in Montana. One day I was working at my desk at the church and the winds started to blow more than usual. In that my office was on the second floor of the educational unit with nothing on the outside to act as a barrier, it wasn't unusual for me to hear and feel the winds, but this was different.

The windows started to shake and move in their frames, and the sound of the wind was loud and frightening. When some of the gusts hit the windows, you could see the panes bending in, as if they were ready to send glass all over my office. I decided that maybe I should go downstairs, get into my car, and go home for the day.

I hadn't traveled more than a block or two when the big wind hit Livingston. Even in my heavy car, I could feel the force of that gust of wind. The car felt as if it were floating on air...and it probably was, for the news later reported that the gust hit 126 mph.

Thankfully, the winds of Montana are generally dry lacking in moisture. If the wind would have had a high moisture content, like a hurricane, the gust of wind would have probably destroyed more property. As it turned out, however, about the only damage that occured was part of the roof was blown off the high school and some private dwellings lost some shingles and a few window panes. Also, a few travel trailers were blown off the highway and some road signs were destroyed, but other than that, the damage was minimal.

Living in Montana you are always prepared for the high winds that come down off the mountain peaks, and in some places like Livingston there are signs placed along the highway warning the traveler of high winds, but not even Livingston was prepared for a wind that reached 126 mph. That even made national news on CBS that evening.

Livingston people are the recipients of some good-natured jokes concerning all the wind that blows in their area. One time I was invited to speak to a group of Park County ranchers and a pastor friend had the responsibility of introducing me to the whole group. He said, "You can always tell where Pastor Johnstad is serving, because they warn you along the highway, "Beware, you are entering a high wind area."

When the winds blow down the Livingston valley in the winter time, the jokes end...especially for those who are knee deep in snow. When the winter winds blow, they sometimes bring the warm air from the coastal area to the west. They are called chinooks. I have seen the temperature move from below zero to 50 degrees above...in a matter of a few hours. I have seen buds appear on trees in February and, yes, some years I even played golf every month.

The former, and now deceased, mayor of Billings, Mayor Frazier had chinooks in mind when he answered the critics of his poor snow removal policy in Billings. He would say, "Let the man who put it there take it away." Billings was on the eastern edge of those winds which came down off the mountains by Livingston.

The point of all I'm trying to say is simply this, the wind blows in Montana. Sometimes it can reach 126 mph, blowing a roof off a house, while at another time it brings a stirring of spring and summer in the middle of winter. It is part of that which makes Montana...Montana.

Catching a Moose

In the fall of the year a group of us from Livingston would make our annual trek to Shoshone and Lewis Lakes in Yellowstone National Park. At this time of year the large German brown trout were traveling out of Shoshone Lake into the Lewis River...a river which ultimately flows into Lewis Lake a few miles to the southeast.

The size of the trout that made that annual trip down the river was enough to stir the blood of any avid fisherman. They could weigh in anywhere from one pound to ten pounds. The trout were strong fighters...solid of flesh and game in spirit. When they surfaced with a fly in the corner of their mouths, the air churned from the explosion of their fanning tails. No understanding fisherman could resist the excitement..

The distance from Livingston to Shoshone Lake trailhead was long ...nearly a hundred miles. A third of those miles were traveled inside the park boundries, where we had to travel slowly due to speed limits and game on the road. The first time I went with the group we left at 4:00 a.m. and arrived at the trailhead as the sun was fully risen in the east.

I shall never forget the beauty of the day. The fall colors had started to linger on the trees and the sound of camp robbers, eagles, and squirrels started to fill the spaces between the quietness of the morning. There was a collection of dew on the grass that sparkled like diamonds from the rays of the sun. On the trail you could clearly see where deer had crossed the path leaving residue that was still warm and steaming.

When the lake first came into view it brought a lump in my throat. The lake was surrounded by huge pine trees that reflected on the surface. It was so calm that I thought someone had taken a large scraper over the entire surface. The calmness was momentarily disrupted by the rising of some mallards on the far end of the lake.

It didn't take me long to get my flyrod rigged and ready for the day's action. In my mind I could feel the initial bump and tug of a big brown as it cradled my woolly worm in its mouth. My fingers trembled with excitement, making it extremely difficult to hold the fly steady as I tried to get the tippet through the eyelet of the fly. Finally, I got the hook and line connected and I stepped gingerly into the water...feeling the chill of the water around my waders.

The other people had moved to other parts of the river and the lake...I was by myself. I carefully worked my way out into the lake, shivering from the cold as the water splashed against my legs. Soon I was where I wanted to be. I started the forward and backward motion with my arm and released the weight forward line at 10 o'clock. The fly landed softly on the surface and moved slowly down the river over a deep hole.

Nothing happened! So I retraced my pattern and released my fly a bit higher up the river than before. This time the fly settled to the surface at the head of the hole and it worked back at even a slower pace. There was a small bump, but the fish didn't really get ahold of it, so I retraced my pattern again, only this time I couldn't get my fly to come forward. Something had caught my fly and held it back. It felt like I had snagged a tree branch near the shoreline.

I couldn't believe my eyes. There, not more than thirty yards behind me stood a huge bull moose...and my fly was caught on its antler. My heart went to my throat. There was no place to go. The lake trapped my escape on three sides and a bull moose trapped me from behind. I thought to myself, "Great, I go to Yellowstone Park to catch a nice trout and what do I get, a bull moose!"

I stood in the lake looking at the moose wondering what I should do. My whole life flashed before my eyes and I could read the obituary column clear as day. "Pastor dies catching a moose in Yellowstone Park."

But someone was watching over me. The moose turned his head and the fly fell off. He looked at me again, made a slight snort, and walked into the woods. Fishing was good the remainder of that day, but I kept watching the shoreline behind me for any stray moose.

Peanut Butter Outback

Let's face it, some people are hooked on hamburgers, some on bacon and eggs, and others on steak or shrimp. As for me, I'm hooked on peanut butter. I always have been ...it goes way back to my childhood.

Mother used to make her famous homemade bread once or twice a week depending on how hungry the children were. We would load up a slice of her bread with butter from the local creamery, add a good bit of peanut butter and homemade blackberry preserves, and then it was topped off with another slice of bread. As children, we lived on it...and loved it!

In fact, peanut butter was once the cause of a family crisis. One day, my brother was commissioned to go to the store and pick up a new jar of peanut butter. We seldom were without peanut butter...even during the war years. While returning home from the store, with the peanut butter jar under his arm, he had to pass by the home of a family who had a very the mischievous son.

Their son enjoyed harassing people, especially if they had our last name. When the harasser confronted my brother on this particular day, my brother accidently dropped the jar on the sidewalk, breaking it into a hundred pieces or more. A mini crisis was born that day.

No person could get away with breaking a jar of peanut butter belonging to our family. Such action demanded revenge...which we got the day we sneaked into the basement of the harasser and mixed up the tracks on his train set. We had the cars moving in every direction by the time we were done. Ultimately, after my father talked to the boy's father, the harasser paid for a new jar of peanut butter, and similar incidents never happened again. I always wondered, why?

With such love for peanut butter, you can probably understand why I had to have peanut butter tucked away in my saddle bags on a three day horse trip into the Boulder River drainage, south of Big Timber. The Roald Mogens from Livingston had invited Mark and I to go with them on a fifty mile horse trip across the mountains into Yellowstone National Park. Roald had planned the menu for the trip. It did not include peanut butter.

We had quite a discussion about the subject prior to making the trip. Roald said that I ought not worry, there would be plenty of food along and I would not starve. I said, "But you don't understand Roald, peanut butter is a way of life." "Sorry," he answered, "you'll just have to live without it for a few days." I said under my breath, "We'll see about that."

The day we departed the campsite on the Boulder River near Box Canyon, I slipped my peanut butter and some bread into my saddle bags. I put it on the bottom of one bag, where it could not be easily detected. As I mounted my gelding, my leg crossed over the bag and it was good.

I was very cautious about eating any of the bread and peanut butter while the others were looking. Once or twice each day I would take up the rear of the string and struggle to get my hand down into the bag without anyone noticing it. That wasn't easy to do, especially while dodging branches or traveling on high mountain trails but if you love peanut butter you get the job done.

As I was munching away on a quicky sandwich, one of the Mogen family happened to turn and catch me in the act. (Crime never pays!) I tried to get the sandwich back into the bag, but when I did, the whole loaf dumped out of the bag onto the ground...including my peanut butter jar.

I heard Roald cry out, "Oh, oh...you brought it with you didn't you?" "Afraid so," I replied. Roald laughed, shook his head, and kept moving up the trail. I was pretty embarrassed when I dismounted and picked up the pieces, but I did it...for I didn't want to lose what was left. After all we still had a day remaining and one day without peanut butter is one day too many.

The peanut butter jar is still in our home even though it doesn't get opened as much as it once did. It is really a true statement, "The older a person gets, the less they eat," but old or not, whenever I get really hungry the peanut butter jar is where I go.

The Chess Challenger

For most of my life I had thought that the game of chess was way over my head. I knew that it was the "Breakfast of Champions" for many people...including kings and paupers, but I never really took an interest in learning the game until I arrived in Billings.

When I lived in Billings, I developed high blood presure and my doctor gave me orders to get into some excercise group to help lower it. I believe he was the one who suggested that I might check out the local YMCA for assistance in finding such a group. He was correct. The local Y had a group that met early in the morning three days a week, so I joined up.

It was here that I met many special people too numerous to mention. There was, however, one person that was to become a very close friend to me, John Thompson, a transplanted Texan.

John was retired from the oil business and had traveled all over the world. His travels took him to Spain where he met his wife Carmen and ultimately to Billings where he ended his career working for an oil company. But John was always a Texan at heart.

John tells the story about how he once bet with someone that he could look over a restaurant crowd and tell who was from Texas in just a few moments. The person took the bet. With that, John stood up and sang the song "The eyes of Texas are Upon You" and people with Texas roots stood up all over the dining area.

John was also an expert chess champion, having started the Texas Chess Tournament (he once played fifty people at the same time and won all fifty games) and a teacher of the game, too. Since his retirement John has formed a chess club in Billings where he continues to teach people how to play the game. He also taught me how to play chess...but privately and under different conditions.

After our exercising was over for the morning and prior to my having to go to work John and I would play chess in the YMCA cafeteria. We played three times a week for nearly eight years. All the while, John had the patience of Job and the wisdom of Solomon as he showed me, again and again, some of the key moves for developing strategy and position on the board. He was forever telling me, "Capture the middle of the board...capture the middle." Whenever I tried, he countered with a move that put my pieces in jeopardy. He is a true genius of the game.

I still play chess with John whenever I travel back to Billings. This past summer we played and for the first time ever I managed to conquer his game. When the game was completed John looked up at me with his piercing eyes and said, "Well done!" I felt that I had just climbed Mt. Everest and made it to the top.

John is also a very active layperson in the Episcopal church. We would often chat about matters of the church...matters that were common to all Christians. We often did this while playing chess...and I have sometimes wondered if he didn't do that purposely to detract me from my game. No matter, his insight into the faith has helped me many times down through the years becoming my mentor, my teacher and my dear friend.

If the reader should ever get to Billings, be sure you get to meet John Thompson. He will be at the "Y" on Monday, Wednesday, and Friday at 6:00 a.m. He will gladly give you a free chess lesson...but beware, you may have to listen to some of his stories too, especially about lawyers and Texans.

Better Believe the Preacher

One of my favorite fishing places in Montana was at Gunner's pond, in Park County. Gunner Westling and his brother were immigrants from Sweden. They moved into Park county and settled on the western slope of the Crazy Mountains. There they built a cow ranch and a pond...a pond that was filled with large trout.

I fished the pond numerous times over the years, and always managed to catch fish. When I moved to Billings I didn't get to fish the pond as much because of the distance factor, but whenever I could, I would! Sometimes if the pace of ministry became overwhelming I would visit the pond just to get life back in its proper perspective.

Gunner's pond was often spoken of in conversations with other fishermen. They kept asking me to take them to the place so that they might see for themselves how good it actually was. Finally they wore me down and I consented to take them to the pond one day.

When the day arrived for the trip a spring snowstorm hit our portion of the state. The reports from the highway department weren't good, but I knew that you couldn't always depend on the accuracy of their reports...especially for the mountainous country where the weather changes every five minutes.

Some of the guys resisted the idea that we should venture out into the storm but I kept encouraging them by saying that it would probably turn out to be a beautiful day, and in that I had a four-wheel drive suburban, not to worry. We would take plenty of emergency equipment with and we would not take foolish chances. We would have a CB radio in the vehicle as well. In the end, they all agreed to go.

Nearly the whole way to Gunner's we fought blowing snow and ice. The ice on the windshield was so thick the blades couldn't keep it cleaned off. The guys took turns stepping out of the vehicle and scraping off the ice.. Although the heater worked well inside the rig, the snow caked up faster than the heat could take off the ice. It appeared that we had made a mistake when we decided to go fishing this day.

The comments being made inside the vehicle were most interesting. Someone said, "Sure, it's going to be a nice day, about the same kind of day General Custer had when he rode into the Big Horn valley." Another person piped up, "It will be a nice day picking ice out of our rod ferrels! Does anyone have an ice auger along?" And then came the closer, "Well, we are with a preacher...keep that it mind! If you can't believe him, who can you believe?"

In spite of the raspberries I continued my words of encouragement. When we finally hit highway 89 to the north, I had to admit that even I had become skeptical. But by the time we had arrived in Clyde Park, about twenty miles from our destination, we suddenly drove out of storm into one of the most beautiful days you could ever imagine.

The vehicle became strangely silent. The shock of what just happened was almost indescribable...no one could believe that the weather could change that quickly. Looking behind us, the two fronts looked as though someone had taken a pencil and drawn a perpendicular line separating the snow line from the sun line to the north. And then just as suddenly the silence was broken by the laughter and hooting of the fishermen in the vehicle. Most of it was coming out of those who had crow in their mouths!

The day turned out beautiful. The sun shone all day; the fish took the bait; and the ride home was less strenuous for the pastor. One of them said, "You know, we'd better believe the preacher from now on!" They all nodded their heads in agreement, and I said to myself, "Thanks, God, you are the one who did it!"

He Paid His Keep

We raised several golden retrievers in our family over the years. Major, the dog mentioned earlier in the book, was the first one. He was followed by a female named Cinnamon that we purchased from a rancher south of Livingston in Cinnabar Basin. Her full name was Cinnamon of Cinnabar Basin, and she was a beautiful dog that whelped two litters of pups for us.

We raised a male pup from one of her litters and we called him Drifter. Drifter should have been called Jumper, because he would leap up on the back of our horses, leap out of his dog pen and probably over the moon...if given the opportunity.

But the unique thing about Drifter was not his leaping ability but his keen sense for money. Whenever Drifter was loose on his own (often jumping over the fence), he would run up into the hills behind our house, find his hidden cache of money, and bring dollar bills back to his kennel. He would drop them in his kennel where you couldn't miss seeing them.

Yes, Drifter knew where there was money planted in the rims behind our house. And there must have been quite a stash, because he didn't bring back just a couple dollars, he brought back several dollars...all at different times and when we weren't watching him. The minute he knew that we were watching him, he would not go to his private stock. No matter how hard we tried to find the cache, Drifter died with the secret in his heart.

I often wondered how much money was still left up in

those rims and who put it there? Did someone rob a bank and hide the money in the rims? Did someone lose their billfold? Was there only dollar bills in the cache, or were there larger bills? We'll probably never know the answer to those questions because of Drifter's death.

My daughter Heidi wrote a theme in school about Drifter. She appropriately entitled it, "My Dog Pays For His Keep." If I remember correctly she received an "A" on her theme.

Geese Galore

A member of my congregation in Billings whispered in my ear one day, "There's geese coming in on my wheat fields every morning from a lake down by Rapelje. If you get there early enough I think you could get some of them. We'd have to dig some pits in the field and cover you with some wheat stubble, but that's no problem."

I turned to him and said, "You mean you know exactly where the geese come in and where to dig the pits?" "Yes," he replied, "and if they continue to follow the pattern they have been keeping, they'll settle on the field about 6:00...sharp!" I replied, "Will tomorrow morning be soon enough?" Laughing, he answered, "I'll have the shovels ready to dig pits about 5:00 tomorrow morning."

Well, let me tell you, I was one busy person the rest of that afternoon and evening. First, I had to get a duck stamp. I normally didn't purchase one when I lived in Billings. Secondly, I had to haul out my hunting equipment and clean my gun...making sure I had proper shells for geese. Thirdly, I had to call someone to go with me, who, when I told him what was about to happen, did not hesitate to accept my invitation.

When the alarm went off...about 3:00 a.m., I jumped out of bed with the thought of geese coming in on my pit in a matter of a few hours. Shortly afterwards my hunting buddy arrived and we headed west out of Billings toward Rapelje. It was 4:00a.m. when we got on the road. Knowing that it was about an hour's drive to the ranch, we figured that we would arrive on time...which we did.

When we arrived, Gary was already up and had the shovels waiting. He drove us down to the field where the geese normally came in. When we arrived at the place, we heard geese honking down by the lake about a mile away. Gary knew that those geese would soon be lifting off the lake and heading for his fields.

We jumped out of the vehicle, grabbed the shovels, and started digging two pits in the field about ten feet apart. When we finished digging them (it didn't take long), the rancher had each of us lay down in one of them. One person faced north, the other south. Our guns were by our side...fully loaded and ready to start shooting at a moments notice.

Gary had been gathering wheat stubble from his field while we were digging the pits. Once we were laying in the pits, he covered us with wheat, making us almost impossible to see. This was extremely important because geese have tremendous eyesight, and they will not settle down where there is a slight prospect of danger.

Gary wished us luck and drove the vehicle back to the ranch. We hadn't been there more than ten minutes when you could hear the geese coming off the lake toward us. We had earlier agreed between us that if the geese came in around us, we would count to ten, shout "now" and jump up shooting. One person would shoot one direction, the other in the opposite direction...for obvious reasons.

The honking of the geese continued to get louder and louder and suddenly they were right over us. The sound of their wings cutting through the air was like a helicopter landing beside you. That sound combined with their honking was unbelieveably awesome...it made goose pimples surface on the back of my neck. When I dared to peek out of my pit there were geese on the ground all around me.

I started counting to ten. When ten came and left, I shouted out the password. The other person had done the same thing...at the same time, for we jumped out of our pits almost simultaneously. There were geese all around us. Some were so close that I could have reached out and caught them by hand. Suddenly the quietness of the morning was shattered by the sound of geese flying and shooters shooting.

The limit on geese was three each day. When the brief encounter between the hunter and the hunted was over (it couldn't have taken more than a minute), each of us had our limit of northern geese. They were the large geese...sometimes called greater geese, with the black head and white bandana under their chin. We estimated that they weighted around ten pounds each.

Shortly after the shooting stopped Gary came down with the vehicle to where we were standing geese in hand. He had a large grin on his face when he said, "How did you do?" I looked at him and said, "I should have had a dozen out of that flock, but I only managed to get three." My partner grinned and said something like, "We didn't do too badly...we only got our limit!"

No person can imagine the thrill of having that many geese land right on top of you. You have to experience it to know the feeling. We were part of the fortunate few people who ever had that experience and it was fantastic. The next best thing to being in on such an experience is hearing it from someone who was there. I was there...and believe me I would like to be there again someday. Who knows, maybe a rancher will whisper in my ear again in church, "There are geese coming in on my fields." Would I go? Would tomorrow morning be soon enough?

The Christmas Surprise

Christmas is always a special time in the church no matter where the church gathers. It is a time for celebrative worship including special music, prayers, gifts, and preaching. At the Lutheran Church of the Good Shepherd in Billings we even hosted a living nativity pageant each year...complete with live animals. Many local people made it a regular part of their Christmas schedule to attend that pageant each year.

Also the church offered three worship events on Christmas eve. The first was a family service at 7:00 p.m., the second was at 9:00 p.m., and the final worship was at ll:00 p.m.   All three of the services offered a candlelighting event, with Holy Communion at the final service. We also held hands and sang "The Lord's Prayer" together...it was a special tradition.

When my daughter Heidi (she played her trumpet at every service) and I returned home after the last service, we were generally exhausted. However we soon forgot how tired we were as we started opening our gifts as a family. After the gifts had been opened, we talked about the gathering of the Johnstad clan that day in Wisconsin.

The Johnstad family gathered at our home in Pigeon Falls each Christmas Day and my mother Olga prepared her annual lutefisk dinner. About sixty or seventy people would generally attend the gathering including brothers, sisters, aunts, uncles, nieces and nephews. It was a special time for our immediate family but we could never attend because of the distance factor. That was about to change.

The juices started to flow when someone suggested that we call the airport to see if we could get a flight back to Wisconsin that morning.   We had to be back to Billings before the following sunday, but we had a few days...if we could get a flight out. We called Northwest Airlines and we could do it...everything fit.

By now it was well after 1 a.m., and we had a lot of things to do before we left Billings at 7:00 a.m. We had to pack (including our Christmas presents), get someone to watch the dog (she also had puppies), and take care of the house.   We also had to figure out how we could get a golden retreiver puppy back to Wisconsin with us.   My brother had spoken for a puppy earlier.   We got everything done and reported to the airport on time.

When we arrived in Minnesota the daughter of my cousin picked us up at the airport and drove us to her home in St. Paul.   When we arrived there I called my mother in Pigeon Falls to tell her that we would sure miss the family reuniion and to greet everyone.   (What I really wanted to know was when everyone was going to gather at the hall in Pigeon Falls.)   She said that everyone should be there by 5:00 p.m. that day, and that she would bring special greetings to the family from us.   As I hung up the phone I said "Eat some lutefisk for me, o.k.?"

My cousin helped me find a Santa Claus outfit to take along on the hundred mile journey from St. Paul to Pigeon Falls.   When we arrived we drove up to my home church and I changed into the Santa outfit.   Then we drove past our home to make sure everyone had left the house for the hall.   Once we were sure that everyone was gathered in the hall, Santa made his appearance.

I walked into the hall and started greeting people, making sure that I disguised my voice. When my brother Conrad saw me, he turned to my brother-in-law Doug Norvold and said "Who is that?" With his dry sense of humor, Doug replied "It's Santa Claus, who do you think?" Neither of them knew, nor suspected in any way, that it was a brother from Montana.

After making sure I had greeted everyone in the hall, I went to the front of the hall and bowed low. When I straightened up with my mask removed the shock on the faces of the people was something to see. No one had the slightest idea who I was, however, my sister-in-law Margaret saw my shoes and thought to herself, "That's Ron!" She was right! Everyone asked, "Where's Mary Ellen, Mark, and Heidi?" I said, "They are out in the car." A couple of nieces and nephews ran out and said, "Come on in, everyone is crying in there." The rest of the family soon joined me, with the puppy in the arms of one of them.

The Johnstad family is known to "cry at the opening of a super market." This was no opening of a super market, this was the opening of a dream. It was something our family never thought would happen. The tears of happiness that flowed that evening will never be forgotten by anyone. It truly made Christmas...Christmas!

Sermons Aren't Boring

The high school choir generally sat to the right of the pulpit at The Lutheran Church of the Good Shepherd in Billings. They would often sing two or three times a month at the early service, and it was always a pleasure to listen to them. Their marvelous talent and enthusiastic spirit always brought joy to any worship event.

Sometimes they would sing at both services on Sunday morning, depending on schedules of choirs, directors, and congregational events. It was on one of those Sundays that I made a huge mistake, I left my sermon in the pulpit between services, and some of the choir members noticed it.

One of the choir members inserted a very interesting picture in the middle section of my manuscript...a centerfold from Playboy magazine...the current issue. I don't recall what subject I was preaching on that day, but I do recall the surprise and the shock I had when I turned one of the pages of my sermon and saw that centerfold looking at me.

I stopped preaching and looked twice at what was in front of me. I couldn't believe it! I asked myself, "How did that get in here?" I must have registered a very shocked and confused look, for the youth immediately started snickering and laughing.

When I looked at them, a few boys had their heads lowered and smiles registered at the corner of their mouths. Actually, it wasn't difficult to know who had done it, for the youth, especially the girls, looked first at me and then at the boys with the smiles. Actually, everyone in the choir was in on the prank...guilt covered the whole choir that day.

They were all waiting for me to turn the page.

I never asked anyone who had done it, nor did I make a big issue out of it. Had I done that, you never knew what might happen next. Those youth were experts at pulling pranks on people and their preacher was no exception.

I learned my lesson well that Sunday. From that day on, I never left my sermon in the pulpit between services...especially when the youth were singing at both services.

The Whoopie Tent

There are all sorts of good tents built for the rugged duty of the Montana mountains. A good tent must be light weight for backpacking or packing on a horse. It must be rain repellent and have a good fly. Also, it must be able to breath air in order that it does not freeze up on the inside. Most of these things did not fit the description of the tent that some of us called the "Whoopie Tent."

Glenn Iverson from Billings owned the tent and he had it all the years I knew him. Several of us from Billings, including Norm and Joanne Ellertson, Van and Cheryl Pittack, Glenn and LaVonne, and my wife, Mary Ellen and I would ride our horses many miles into the depths of the Montana mountains and take turns staying in that two person tent.

The tent was a small mountaineer with barely enough room for two people. It was larger on one end than on the other. You entered the tent feet first and slept with your feet toward the narrow end. Just getting your bag inside the tent was difficult enough, but when you had to get into your bag once it was inside the tent you had to be part snake.

The inside of the tent shrunk quickly when a "mucho grande hombre" entered it along with his wife and his saddle. The saddle was put inside the tent for two reasons: one, to keep it dry, and two, to be used as a pillow . Of course, the saddle also blocked the entrance to the tent. You had to find your most comfortable position to sleep because there would be no getting up once you were settled down for the night. You couldn't roll over without waking

117

up the other person or suffocating them.

Something told me that it was going to be a long night and I was right. I had just fallen asleep when I heard the wind starting to blow and the sound of raindrops splattering on the tent. Then it happened...the tent partially collapsed. Whenever I would take a breath I would nearly suck the tent lining into my mouth.

Once I found my boots at the bottom of the tent, I managed to slip them on and wriggle my way out into the rain. It is not one of the most enjoyable camping experiences to have to redo your tent in the middle of a rainstorm...but I managed to get it done and wormed my way back inside the tent.

I pulled the zipper on my bag, shivering from the cold and was just going back to sleep when nature called...and called quite loudly. So it was up again and out into the wind and rain. After completing my chores I slithered back into the tent for the third time.

Just as I started to doze off, I heard the horses start to stomp their hoofs, let out some whinny sounds, and then move back and forth on the line we had strung between two trees. Although we had the food strung up on one of the branches of a tree, I knew that we were being visited by some local bears. Once again I wriggled my way to the outside.

As I carefully moved in the direction of the horses, clad only in my underwear and carrying a flashlight it occured to me how ridiculous I must have looked and how stupid. I thought to myself, "What can you do to a bear with a flashlight? You don't have anything along to defend yourself should you get yourself into trouble with a bear." I quickly shined the light toward the horses and, seeing nothing unusual...like a set of eyes closer to the ground, I headed back to the tent for the fourth time.

By now the night was well spent and I had managed to catch maybe an hour's sleep.   I knew that it was useless for me to go back inside the tent to sleep, so I carefully and quietly rummaged around inside the tent for my boots and trousers.   Once finding them I threw them outside where it would be easier to put them on, grabbed my saddle, and went down by the lake to build a fire.

Soon the fire was burning brightly, and the warmth of it filled the area. I positioned my saddle alongside the fire so that I would be able to lie down and have the heat cover my cold and tired body.   I filled up the coffee pot and tucked it into the fire before I lay down. As I waited for the coffee to brew the words of my wife came to mind.   She would say, "My idea of camping is a Holiday Inn, complete with heat, hot water, and a warm bed."   At that point I would have agreed with her.

Shortly thereafter the coffee was done and the sun started coming up in the east.   The colors provided by the morning light changed from one degree of blue to another...with flashes of orange and red mixed into the middle of picture.   Some fish were already starting to rise for breakfast and several ducks were seen flying toward my fire...staying close to the surface of the lake.

As I reached for my flyrod, dreaming about the trout that would soon fill the frying pan, a person emerged from the larger tent saying "How did you sleep?" "Fine," I lied, as I continued to drink my coffee and fumble with my flyrod. Somehow I knew that she didn't believe me, and she was right. I was really happy that it would be someone else's turn in the Whoopie Tent on our next outing.

The Treasure Hunt

At Rimrock Mall in Billings, seventy merchants decided to hold a promotional event to coincide with the opening of the mall. It was an innovative promotional...a treasure hunt where each of the merchants offered a clue to the solving of the hunt. The person who first unraveled all the clues would win one thousand silver dollars.

I was out of town on church business the Saturday that it was held, but my wife and daughter Heidi plus my wife's parents, got to the mall the minute it opened. Heidi immediately started going from store to store picking up each clue and working feverishly to fit one clue with the next. She didn't even stop for lunch, she was too engrossed in the process.

Later in the afternoon, she told her mother, "I think I know where the treasure is being kept." She pointed outside the mall to the Rimrock Bank across the street and said, "It's there, in the bank."

So they walked over to the bank and when the person said, "My I help you?", Heidi replied, "Yes, I think you are holding the thousand silver dollars here for the treasure hunt at the mall." The lady answered, "Just a moment please." and scurried off.

When she returned, she had the president of the bank with her and he said, "So you think we have the treasure here for the hunt going on in the mall, is that correct?" Heidi looked at him and said, "Yes, I do." "Well," he replied, "come with me and we'll take a look."

They went into the vault area and he proceeded to take a key and open one of the lock boxes. When Heidi was invited to look inside, there were one thousand silver dollars facing her. She had unraveled all the clues before numerous people twice her age (she was eleven at the time) even came close to solving the mystery.

The Billings Gazette took a picture of her smiling over a table with fifty pounds of silver coins in bags planted in front of her. She was one happy young lady...and excited that she had beaten everyone to the treasure.

When I returned to Billings that evening I was picked up by my father-in-law and he was quieter than usual. I shrugged it off, thinking he was having a bad day. But as we got closer to my home he got even quieter, so I said, "What's going on, aren't you feeling well?" "It's nothing," he replied, "I'm just tired from a long day of shopping with your family."

When we arrived home I walked into the house and was greeted by my mother-in-law, Heidi (with a cap on her head), and Mary Ellen sitting at the table with playing cards in their hands. By each of them were stacks of silver dollars, empty beer cans from our neighbors, and silver dollars in the middle of the table. I couldn't believe my eyes. They had changed the preacher's house into a gambling casino.

"Where did all those silver dollars come from?" I asked. Everyone started to laugh as they explained to me what had happened that day at the mall. I looked at Heidi and said, "Wow, am I proud of you...what a girl!"

Before Heidi put them in a safe place she took ten percent, a tithe, or one hundred silver dollars, and put fifty of them into the Sunday school offering the next day and fifty into the offering plate during worship. She decided to do this on her own, without any prompting from her mother or her father. She knew the importance of steward-ship...and taught others the importance of it as well.

It Took Six Cans

There's a story from one of the books of the Bible, the book of John, where six cans of water turned a wedding feast into a joyous event. The water was changed into wine by Jesus and then served to the guests at the conclusion of the marriage celebration. Jesus had saved the host from embarrassment with those six cans (jars) of wine. (A Jewish wedding always provided enough wine for everyone.)

My wife saved an embarrassed husband with six cans of tomato juice, but first the story. While I was hunting pheasants and walking through some tall grass I suddenly smelled a terrible odor around me. It smelled just like strong onions and like onions it made my eyes water.

The smell was so bad that I had to turn into the wind to drive the smell away from me. I had been sprayed...close up...by a skunk. I never saw the creature, but the evidence was clearly established. I had a new kind of after shave lotion added to my body.

The return trip home was a long one. My hunting friend had his window open most of the way...and it was cold outside. My dog whined and wanted to put his face out a window too. He breathed a sigh of relief when I opened the window for him. As for me I had grown accustomed to the smell.

Arriving at my domicile, my wife caught the first whiff said, "Get those clothes off immediately and hit the shower." I took them off in the garage and escaped to the shower. Meanwhile, she jumped into her car (my truck smelled a bit rank) and headed for the grocery store to buy tomato juice.

Returning from the store, loaded down with six large cans of juice she held her breath, turned off the shower, and started to pour tomato juice over my head. She broke out in laughter, watching the juice flow down and over my body. I must have looked like I was bleeding from a massive wound...arrayed in my birthday suit.

Slowly but surely the smell started to disappear and I was free at last! (The parishioners to whom I served communion the next morning must have been grateful.) The clothes received a similar treatment from my wonderful wife. After soaking in tomato juice for several days, then washed, they recovered equally well.

Be careful when you go hunting in Montana, you never know when you might get skunked.

A Big Horn Experience

Probably one of the best fishing streams in Montana is the Big Horn River, south of Billings, at Fort Smith. Several years ago, a large dam was constructed at the Fort which made the river below the dam a controlled environment for some of the best trout fishing in the world and the lake above a recreationalists paradise...with some excellent walleye fishing thrown in.

The several occasions I have had to float the river in a Mackenzie boat and to wade some of the magnificent downstream pools with my 8' graphite fly rod in hand and a local fly pattern tied to my tippet, were never a disappointment to me. I often caught and released rainbow or brown trout in the 2-3 pound class. On occasion you could expect a real lunker to attack your fly, but with increased pressure from fishing people those strikes are getting harder to come by.

Above the dam where water has been backed up for several miles into Wyoming fishing is excellent...especially for walleyed pike. People who know what the lake produces will travel for miles to toss a quarter ounce yellow and white jig up to the shoreline and jig it back to the boat...anticipating a strike from the fish with the blank eyes or possibly a small-mouth bass.

Again, it is something that I have done on several occasions and thoroughly enjoyed "most" of the experiences. I say "most" because there was one time that I should have stayed home. Early one spring, I was invited to go with a friend and his buddy down to the lake for some early walleye fishing. They told me that the snow was almost all gone and access to the lake was now possible. Besides he had just purchased a new inboard 23' boat and wanted to take it out for its' maiden cruise. He said he needed a preacher along to bless his new vessel. I grimaced at his invitation, but accepted it anyway.

The trip down to the boat launch near Fort Smith was uneventful. Indeed the snow was nearly gone and we had little trouble getting the boat down the launch pad into the lake. We were all excited when the boat performed better than expected. We soon had traveled several miles down the lake while thinking about the fish that awaited our arrival. Suddenly however things started to change.

First the weather changed. The temperature dropped considerably and snow started to fall so that we could barely see the shoreline from the middle of the lake. We decided to head to shore, eat our lunch, and wait out the storm in the comfort of the boat's cabin. We spent much of the time laughing at ourselves for being out in a boat...miles from nowhere...in the middle of a spring storm. We talked about how isolated we were and how even the authorities knew nothing of our being on the lake. Each of us chuckled at that thought.

After an hour or so of waiting we decided that the storm was not going to let up so we chose to head back to the launch area....10 or 12 miles from where the storm had caught us. When we shoved away from the bank we noticed the boat was very sluggish and appeared to be sitting lower in the water. When my friend hit the throttle the boat did not respond as expected. The bow was pointed to the sky and water started gushing in at the stern.

I grabbed a life preserver and threw myself on the bow

of the boat while the other men started to bail water and toss things over the side that wouldn't be needed. Out on the bow with the cold wind and water whipping up in my face I envisioned myself soon swimming for my life. With no shoreline to land on, no dry matches, no one knowing we were in the area, and no food to eat, our future didn't look good. My life flashed before my eyes and I could hear the bells tolling.

Then we got a break. We decided to throw all our weight toward the bow of the boat while pushing the trottle to the maximum position. So I pulled myself up to a pushup position and waited for the signal. When my friend yelled, "Now!", I threw my 240 pounds down on the bow and felt the jolt of the other men hitting the front of the cabin at the same time.

The boat jerked...bringing the prop out of the water. But it quickly settled back into the lake...gaining momentum in the process. Soon we were moving slowly in the direction of the place where the whole day started. When I saw the boat launching area ahead, I breathed a bit easier, but I didn't get a full breath until we had the vessel up on the trailer.

When we hooked up the boat and started to winch it up on the trailer, we saw what the problem was. My friend had not put the drain plug into the boat before we left the dock. The whole time we were gone it was taking on water and the weight was so great that it nearly brought the boat to the bottom of the lake. An innocent mistake nearly cost us our lives.

Fatting the Preacher

When I first came to Montana I probably weighed 215 pounds and could still run the hundred yard dash in a respectable time. But the Montana women like to fatten up their preachers and keep them looking healthy. They like to feed them bread and rolls made from Montana grain products because there is power in it...the kind of power that stays with you.

The word had gotten out all over four counties that I really liked cinnamon rolls. It must have started in Big Timber at Frys restaurant where they made some of the better cinnamon rolls in Montana. Someone must have either seen me in there enjoying their rolls, or heard me comment about them, because the word soon passed around that I liked them. Before you knew it, I had three or four ladies baking them for me.

The first lady was Ed Swandal's wife Borghild in Wilsall. She not only made excellent cinnamon rolls but she also made some of the best bread in the country. Many times when we drove out to the ranch to visit, Borghild would have rolls, brown bread, fresh jam and coffee for us. And occasionally when she baked, she would have one of her family members bring freshly baked bread and rolls into town for us too. The Swandals always made sure you had enough to eat. Borghild also did our family another important deed she taught my wife how to make that brown bread and lefse too!

The second lady who baked for me was Ole Fallon's wife, Kristina. (Ole was a pioneer legislator from Park County.) Kristina not only fed me great rolls while I was serving the congregation in Livingston, but when I moved to another church in Billings she would send rolls over to me with her daughter Gloria who lived in Billings at that time. Kristina always made sure that her former pastor was never forgotten. What a blessing she was!

Then there was also Margaret Tjeltveidt from Red Lodge. She was another one who kept the preacher on the heavy side. She even welcomed me to Billings with a whole pan of goodies on my first day on the job at The Lutheran Church of the Good Shepherd. Imagine, if you will, driving to Billings to leave goodies for me even though she didn't attend my church. But that's a Montanan for you...they care about people.

There was one other person that kept me gaining weight while I lived in Montana. I already mentioned her name in the article on hunting pheasants in this book...Gracie Mosdal. Gracie Mosdal made the best...the absolute best ...cinnamon rolls that I have ever tasted.

The rolls were big, moist, and smothered with caramel on the bottom and frosting on the top. There was just enough cinnamon woven between the layers to not make the taste offensive. She would serve them warm, along with fresh butter. If a prize were ever offered at the Yellowstone County Fair for the best cinnamon rolls in the country, Gracie's rolls would have won it every year.

Gracie Mosdal also was known to do things that were rather unique and interesting. For instance, Gracie wrote a book on how to cook with snow. She was suffering from cabin fever one winter and decided that she should spend some of her day developing recipes for those who experienced similar circumstances. It was funny...and people

131

bought them all over Montana.

Gracie also knew that cinnamon rolls were special on my list. A couple times while I was serving on the Synod Council and had to travel from Billings to Great Falls I would leave early and go through Broadview. Gracie would get up early in the morning, bake the cinnamon rolls, and then get into her car and drive to Broadview...about ten miles. There she would leave the pan of rolls on the co-op gas pumps for me to pick up as I went through town. She even left butter, a plastic knife, and napkins.

It's no wonder that I gained weight while serving churches in Montana. When I left Montana for El Paso, Texas, nearly twenty years later, I weighed in at 240 pounds. I'm still not sure what preachers are worth per pound.